Costa]

Everything You Need to Know

2

Introduction to Costa Rica: A Pura Vida Paradise

Nestled in the heart of Central America, Costa Rica beckons travelers with its breathtaking natural beauty, vibrant culture, and a way of life that embodies the phrase "Pura Vida." As we embark on this journey through the captivating tapestry of Costa Rica, let's begin with an introduction to this remarkable paradise.

Costa Rica, often referred to as the "Rich Coast" in Spanish, is a nation that defies its small size by offering a wealth of diverse experiences. Covering just 51,100 square kilometers (19,700 square miles), this tiny country packs an astonishing variety of landscapes, from pristine beaches along its Pacific and Caribbean coasts to lush rainforests, towering volcanoes, and mist-shrouded cloud forests. It's a land of contrasts, where you can bask in the tropical sun on a pristine beach in the morning and find yourself exploring a cool, mossy forest in the afternoon.

The term "Pura Vida" is more than just a slogan in Costa Rica; it's a way of life. Translated as "pure life" or "simple life," Pura Vida represents the essence of the Costa Rican spirit. It's an attitude that values happiness, well-being, and the appreciation of life's simple pleasures. Whether you're savoring a cup of freshly brewed Costa Rican coffee or gazing at the breathtaking Arenal Volcano, you'll quickly realize that this philosophy permeates every corner of the country. Costa Rica is a naturalist's dream come true, boasting a remarkable 5% of the world's biodiversity within its borders. It's a haven for eco-tourism, with over 30 national parks, wildlife reserves, and protected areas that harbor an astounding array of flora and fauna. From the resplendent quetzal, a colorful bird revered by the indigenous cultures, to the elusive jaguar prowling in the depths of the Osa Peninsula, Costa Rica is a sanctuary for nature enthusiasts and wildlife lovers.

History has woven a rich tapestry in this land. The first inhabitants of Costa Rica were indigenous peoples like the Bribri, Cabécar, and Boruca, each with their unique traditions and languages. The arrival of Spanish explorers in the 16th century marked the beginning of a colonial era that left an indelible mark on the country's culture and architecture. Costa Rica's path to independence was a peaceful one, setting it apart from its tumultuous neighbors in Central America.

In the modern era, Costa Rica has carved a niche for itself as a stable and progressive nation. It abolished its army in 1949, a decision that has allowed it to allocate resources to education, healthcare, and environmental conservation. The result is a nation with a high standard of living, universal healthcare, and a strong commitment to sustainability.

As we delve deeper into the chapters of this book, we'll explore the diverse landscapes, uncover the secrets of Costa Rican cuisine, and delve into the depths of its history, culture, and language. We'll traverse the bustling streets of San Jose, hike through pristine rainforests, and share in the rhythms of Costa Rican music and dance. Whether you're planning a visit or simply curious about this enchanting country, join us on this journey as we uncover everything you need to know about Costa Rica, the Pura Vida paradise.

Geographical Wonders: Costa Rica's Diverse Landscapes

Costa Rica's geographical wonders are a testament to the extraordinary diversity that this small Central American country holds within its borders. From the moment you set foot in Costa Rica, you'll be awestruck by the sheer variety of landscapes that unfold before your eyes.

The Pacific and Caribbean coasts, with their miles of pristine beaches, are a natural starting point for any exploration of Costa Rica. The Pacific coast, stretching over 1,290 kilometers (800 miles), offers a wealth of beach experiences, from the bustling surf towns of Tamarindo and Jaco to the secluded and tranquil shores of the Nicoya Peninsula. Whether you're a surfer seeking the perfect wave or simply looking to unwind on the soft sands, the Pacific coast has something for everyone.

On the opposite side of the country lies the Caribbean coast, a place where reggae beats blend with the rustling palms. The towns of Puerto Limón and Puerto Viejo exude a laid-back Caribbean vibe that's worlds apart from the Pacific. Here, you can explore the vibrant Afro-Caribbean culture, savor delicious coconut-infused dishes, and even witness nesting sea turtles in Tortuguero National Park.

As you venture inland, the geography of Costa Rica takes a dramatic turn. The backbone of the country is formed by a chain of volcanic mountains that stretches from the northwest to the southeast. Among them, Arenal Volcano, with its perfectly symmetrical shape, and the imposing Poás Volcano are just a couple of the striking examples of

Costa Rica's volcanic wonders. These volcanoes not only shape the landscape but also provide geothermal energy and hot springs for relaxation.

But it's not just the volcanoes that captivate; it's the lush rainforests that drape over the mountains, creating a verdant paradise. Costa Rica is home to several cloud forests, including the world-famous Monteverde Cloud Forest Reserve. These mystical forests are shrouded in mist and teeming with unique flora and fauna, including the resplendent quetzal and elusive jaguars.

The Osa Peninsula, often called the "most biologically intense place on Earth" by National Geographic, is a treasure trove of biodiversity. Here, you'll find Corcovado National Park, a place where dense primary rainforests meet untouched beaches, and where tapirs, scarlet macaws, and howler monkeys roam freely.

In the northern reaches of Costa Rica, the Guanacaste region boasts a contrasting landscape, with dry tropical forests and savannas. The Palo Verde National Park and the Rincon de la Vieja National Park offer a glimpse into this unique ecosystem, where you can spot crocodiles, exotic birds, and thermal mud pots.

And let's not forget the waterways that crisscross the country. Costa Rica is known for its extensive river systems and pristine lakes, making it a paradise for kayakers and rafters. The Pacuare River is world-renowned for its thrilling white-water rafting adventures, while Lake Arenal provides a picturesque backdrop for windsurfing and fishing.

In this chapter, we've merely scratched the surface of Costa Rica's geographical wonders. The beauty of this country lies in its ever-changing landscapes, from the misty highlands to the sun-drenched beaches, and from the lush rainforests to the arid savannas. As we continue our journey through the chapters of this book, you'll delve deeper into each facet of Costa Rica's remarkable geography, uncovering the secrets of this diverse and captivating land.

The Rich Tapestry of Costa Rican History

The rich tapestry of Costa Rican history weaves a captivating narrative that spans centuries and encompasses a multitude of cultures, events, and transformations. From its earliest indigenous inhabitants to its emergence as a modern, peaceful nation, Costa Rica's history is a story of resilience, progress, and the pursuit of a unique national identity.

Long before the arrival of European explorers, Costa Rica was inhabited by various indigenous groups, each with its distinct languages, customs, and traditions. Tribes like the Bribri, Cabécar, and Boruca inhabited the lush rainforests and fertile valleys, leaving behind traces of their rich heritage in the form of petroglyphs and archaeological sites.

The arrival of Christopher Columbus in 1502 marked the first European contact with this land. However, it wasn't until the early 16th century that Spanish conquistadors, lured by tales of gold and riches, began to explore and establish settlements in Costa Rica. They encountered a challenging terrain and resilient indigenous populations, which made Costa Rica less attractive for large-scale colonization and resource extraction compared to other regions in the Americas.

Costa Rica's colonial history was marked by relative isolation from the centers of Spanish power in the Americas. Its economy primarily revolved around small-scale farming and cattle ranching, rather than the extraction

11

of precious metals. This isolation allowed for a unique blend of Spanish and indigenous cultures to flourish, contributing to the development of a distinctive Costa Rican identity.

In 1821, Costa Rica, along with several Central American provinces, declared its independence from Spain and became a part of the Mexican Empire. However, this affiliation was short-lived, and in 1823, Costa Rica joined the United Provinces of Central America, a federation of Central American states. The federation's dissolution in 1838 marked the beginning of Costa Rica's independent history as a sovereign nation.

Costa Rica's path to nationhood was marked by political stability and a commitment to democracy. The country abolished its army in 1949, a bold move that allowed it to allocate resources to education, healthcare, and social programs. This decision laid the foundation for the nation's reputation as a peaceful and progressive society.

In the latter half of the 20th century, Costa Rica became a hotspot for international conservation efforts, thanks to its commitment to preserving its rich biodiversity. The establishment of a robust national park system, including Corcovado and Tortuguero, solidified Costa Rica's reputation as an eco-tourism paradise.

As the years rolled on, Costa Rica continued to evolve. It became a hub for technology and ecotourism, attracting travelers from around the world who were drawn to its lush landscapes, abundant wildlife, and commitment to sustainability.

Indigenous Peoples of Costa Rica: Past and Present

The history of Costa Rica is intricately entwined with the presence and legacy of its indigenous peoples. From the earliest inhabitants to the present-day indigenous communities, their presence has left an indelible mark on the cultural and social fabric of this vibrant nation.

Costa Rica's indigenous history dates back thousands of years, with archaeological evidence indicating that various indigenous groups inhabited the region long before the arrival of European settlers. Among these groups were the Bribri, Cabécar, Boruca, Ngäbe-Buglé, and many others. Each group had its unique languages, traditions, and ways of life, deeply connected to the diverse ecosystems they called home.

The Bribri and Cabécar, for example, resided in the dense rainforests of the Talamanca Mountains in the southeastern part of Costa Rica. They practiced subsistence agriculture, cultivating crops like maize, cacao, and plantains, while also relying on hunting and gathering to sustain their communities.

In the southwestern region, the Boruca people thrived in the lush highlands and rainforests. They were known for their intricate, handwoven textiles and distinctive balsa wood masks used in traditional ceremonies and festivals.

The Ngäbe-Buglé, predominantly found in the southern part of the country, were skilled in agriculture, crafting intricate baskets, and maintaining a strong sense of communal life. Their language, Ngäbere, is still spoken by their descendants today.

The arrival of Spanish explorers in the early 16th century marked a significant turning point in the history of Costa Rica's indigenous populations. While some indigenous communities resisted Spanish colonization, others were influenced by European culture and religion, leading to a blending of traditions.

Throughout the colonial period, indigenous communities faced challenges such as forced labor and diseases brought by the Spanish, which decimated their populations. However, many resiliently preserved their languages, customs, and spiritual practices.

In recent years, Costa Rica has taken steps to recognize and protect the rights of its indigenous peoples. The country's constitution recognizes the cultural and territorial rights of indigenous communities, and there have been efforts to support indigenous education and healthcare.

Today, Costa Rica's indigenous peoples continue to play an essential role in the country's cultural diversity. They maintain a connection to their ancestral lands, and their traditions are celebrated through festivals, art, and music. Indigenous languages, while facing challenges, are still spoken, and there are ongoing efforts to document and preserve them.

In conclusion, the indigenous peoples of Costa Rica have a rich and resilient history that spans millennia. Their presence and contributions to the country's cultural mosaic are significant and enduring.

Colonial Era and the Spanish Influence

The colonial era of Costa Rica's history was marked by the arrival of Spanish explorers and the enduring influence of Spanish culture and governance on the region. This period, spanning several centuries, left an indelible mark on the nation we know today.

In the early 16th century, Spanish explorers, including Christopher Columbus and Gil González Dávila, arrived on the shores of Costa Rica, drawn by the tales of wealth and potential conquest. However, unlike some other regions in the Americas, Costa Rica did not yield the riches of gold and silver that the Spanish coveted. Instead, it presented formidable challenges, such as rugged terrain, dense rainforests, and a lack of substantial indigenous populations to subjugate.

This lack of immediate wealth led to Costa Rica being relatively neglected by the Spanish crown. The settlers who did arrive faced the challenges of carving out a livelihood in a land that didn't yield the expected treasures. Instead, they turned to subsistence agriculture, cultivating crops such as maize, beans, and cacao. Cattle ranching also became a vital part of the economy, laying the foundation for Costa Rica's cattle culture, which endures to this day.

Costa Rica's relative isolation from the centers of Spanish power in the Americas allowed for a unique cultural and social development. The settlers intermingled with indigenous populations, and over time, a mestizo (mixed-

15

race) society emerged. This blending of cultures contributed to the development of a distinct Costa Rican identity, one that incorporated elements of Spanish and indigenous heritage.

Throughout the colonial period, the Catholic Church played a significant role in shaping the culture and society of Costa Rica. The construction of churches and religious missions became focal points of many communities, and Catholicism left a lasting influence on the spiritual and moral values of the population.

The Spanish colonial era was also marked by the introduction of new crops and animals, transforming the landscape and the way of life. European fruits, vegetables, and livestock, such as cattle, horses, and pigs, were introduced to Costa Rica, forever altering its agriculture and cuisine.

Costa Rica remained a remote and sparsely populated Spanish colony, distant from the major colonial centers of Mexico and Central America. As a result, it experienced less direct Spanish control and intervention. This relative autonomy allowed for a level of self-governance and independence that would later contribute to the nation's democratic traditions.

The colonial period in Costa Rica's history was not characterized by the grandeur and conquest seen in other parts of the Americas. Instead, it was marked by resilience, adaptation, and the emergence of a unique cultural identity. The legacy of Spanish influence can still be seen today in the language, religion, and traditions of Costa Ricans, as well as in the enduring spirit of a nation that values peace, democracy, and cultural diversity.

Costa Rica's Path to Independence

Costa Rica's path to independence is a story of determination, strategic alliances, and the pursuit of self-governance in a complex geopolitical landscape. As we delve into this chapter, we'll uncover the remarkable journey of how Costa Rica emerged as an independent nation.

The road to independence for Costa Rica began in the early 19th century when the winds of change were sweeping across Latin America. At that time, Costa Rica was part of the Captaincy General of Guatemala, a Spanish colony that included much of Central America and Mexico. In 1821, news of Mexican independence from Spain inspired a desire for self-determination among Central American provinces.

On September 15, 1821, the leaders of various Central American provinces, including Costa Rica, gathered in Guatemala City and signed the Act of Independence of Central America. This act declared their separation from Spanish rule and their intent to form a federation of sovereign states.

However, the newly independent Central American provinces soon faced internal divisions and struggles for power. This initial attempt at federation, known as the United Provinces of Central America, proved unstable, leading to political turmoil and regional conflicts.

Costa Rica, with its tradition of relative peace and autonomy, found itself at odds with the more centralized and authoritarian leadership of the federation. The country's leaders, including figures like Juan Mora Fernández, advocated for greater local autonomy and self-governance.

In 1838, following a period of unrest and disputes, the United Provinces of Central America dissolved, and Costa Rica became a fully sovereign nation. This separation marked the beginning of Costa Rica's independent history as a republic.

One significant event during this period was the Battle of Ochomogo in 1823 when Costa Rican forces, led by Juan Mora Fernández, successfully defended their sovereignty against Nicaraguan forces. This battle is often cited as a symbol of Costa Rica's determination to maintain its independence.

Costa Rica's path to independence was marked by its commitment to democracy and the rule of law. The country adopted a constitution in 1825, establishing a republican form of government with checks and balances. This commitment to democratic values would shape the nation's political identity for generations to come.

Over the years, Costa Rica continued to evolve as a peaceful and politically stable nation. In 1949, following a brief civil war, the country took the extraordinary step of abolishing its military, redirecting resources toward education, healthcare, and social welfare programs. This decision solidified Costa Rica's reputation as a haven of peace and democracy.

Modern Costa Rica: A Democratic Success Story

The modern history of Costa Rica is nothing short of a democratic success story that has captivated the world. This tiny nation, nestled in the heart of Central America, has defied the odds to become a shining example of peace, stability, and progressive governance.

Costa Rica's journey to modernity can be traced back to the mid-20th century when it made a pivotal decision that would set it apart from many other nations in the region. In 1949, following a brief but intense civil war, Costa Rica made the bold and visionary move to abolish its military. This historic decision was enshrined in its constitution, making it the first and only nation in the world to do so.

The abolishment of the military was a radical step, especially in a region where military power often played a central role in politics. Instead of allocating resources to a standing army, Costa Rica redirected its funds toward education, healthcare, and social programs. This investment in human capital laid the foundation for a strong and educated workforce, contributing to the country's economic development.

The absence of a military also created a unique political environment. Costa Rica embraced democratic principles and a commitment to the rule of law. Its political landscape became characterized by regular and peaceful transitions of power, a robust multiparty system, and a strong respect for human rights. This democratic stability has endured for decades and is a testament to the country's commitment to fostering an inclusive and participatory society.

Costa Rica's investment in education and healthcare has yielded remarkable results. The country boasts high literacy rates and a well-educated population. It has also developed a robust healthcare system, offering universal healthcare to its citizens and residents. This commitment to the well-being of its people has contributed to the country's high standard of living and long life expectancy.

In the latter part of the 20th century and into the 21st century, Costa Rica positioned itself as a global leader in environmental conservation. The country established a network of national parks and protected areas, preserving its rich biodiversity and natural beauty. These efforts have made Costa Rica a premier destination for eco-tourism and a model for sustainable practices worldwide.

The nation's commitment to environmental conservation extends to its renewable energy initiatives. Costa Rica has made substantial investments in clean energy sources such as hydroelectric, wind, and solar power. As a result, it has been able to generate the majority of its electricity from renewable sources, reducing its carbon footprint and contributing to global efforts to combat climate change.

Moreover, Costa Rica has become a haven for research and innovation. It boasts a growing knowledge economy, with a focus on technology, biotechnology, and other emerging industries. This has attracted international investment and positioned the country as a regional leader in innovation and entrepreneurship.

In summary, modern Costa Rica is a democratic success story that has captured the world's attention. Its decision to abolish the military, invest in education and healthcare, and prioritize environmental conservation has created a model of development that resonates globally.

Biodiversity Beyond Compare: Costa Rica's Flora and Fauna

Costa Rica's biodiversity is nothing short of extraordinary, earning it a reputation as a global hotspot for wildlife and ecological diversity. As we dive into this chapter, you'll come to appreciate the sheer richness and uniqueness of Costa Rica's flora and fauna.

This tiny country, covering just 0.03% of the Earth's landmass, boasts nearly 5% of the world's known biodiversity. To put it into perspective, Costa Rica's land area is smaller than West Virginia, yet it houses a mind-boggling array of species, both plant and animal.

One of the most remarkable aspects of Costa Rica's biodiversity is its astounding variety of ecosystems, ranging from pristine beaches to towering cloud forests, dense rainforests, and volcanic landscapes. This diverse terrain provides numerous niches for an astonishing array of flora and fauna to thrive.

In Costa Rica, you'll encounter a kaleidoscope of species. Among the most iconic are the resplendent quetzal, a vibrantly colored bird revered by indigenous cultures; the three-toed sloth, a master of slow-motion in the treetops; and the red-eyed tree frog, an emblematic symbol of Central American rainforests.

The country is also home to numerous big cats, including jaguars, ocelots, and pumas, which roam the lush forests. In the coastal regions, you can spot sea turtles nesting on pristine beaches, an awe-inspiring sight during nesting season.

Costa Rica's waters teem with marine life, making it a haven for divers and snorkelers. You can swim alongside colorful coral reefs, observe majestic manta rays, and encounter gentle giants like whale sharks and humpback whales during their migrations.

The diversity isn't limited to the animal kingdom; Costa Rica's flora is equally captivating. The country's lush rainforests are adorned with a plethora of orchids, bromeliads, and epiphytes that create a botanical wonderland. Tropical hardwood trees like the magnificent ceiba and the towering kapok are integral to the rainforest ecosystem.

Furthermore, Costa Rica's rivers, lakes, and wetlands are home to an array of aquatic plants, while its cloud forests are characterized by mosses, ferns, and a unique variety of moss-covered trees.

Central to Costa Rica's commitment to conservation is the extensive system of national parks and reserves. Over 25% of the country's land is protected, preserving crucial habitats for its wildlife. Parks like Corcovado, Tortuguero, and Manuel Antonio are renowned for their incredible biodiversity and draw visitors from around the world.

The country's dedication to environmental preservation extends to sustainable tourism and research initiatives. It has become a hub for scientific studies, attracting researchers and students eager to explore its ecosystems and contribute to global knowledge about biodiversity.

Exploring Costa Rica's National Parks and Reserves

Exploring Costa Rica's national parks and reserves is an unparalleled journey into some of the most pristine and diverse ecosystems on the planet. This chapter will take you on a virtual tour through the natural wonders that await within these protected areas.

Costa Rica's commitment to conservation is vividly reflected in its extensive network of national parks and reserves, covering more than 25% of the country's land area. These protected areas are a testament to the nation's dedication to preserving its rich biodiversity, stunning landscapes, and unique habitats.

One of the crown jewels of Costa Rica's national park system is Corcovado National Park. Located on the Osa Peninsula, it's often hailed as one of the most biologically intense places on Earth by National Geographic. Here, you can venture deep into pristine rainforests, home to endangered species like jaguars, tapirs, and scarlet macaws.

Tortuguero National Park, on the Caribbean coast, offers a vastly different but equally captivating experience. Known as the "Land of Turtles," it's a crucial nesting site for green sea turtles, leatherbacks, and hawksbills. Witnessing a sea turtle laying her eggs under the moonlight is a once-in-a-lifetime experience.

Manuel Antonio National Park, located on the Pacific coast, boasts lush rainforests that meet stunning white-sand beaches. Here, you can explore a variety of hiking trails, encounter playful squirrel monkeys, and relax on pristine beaches with gentle waves lapping at the shore.

Arenal Volcano National Park, in the northern region, offers a dramatic backdrop of the iconic Arenal Volcano. Visitors can hike around the base of the volcano, soak in natural hot springs, and admire the abundant birdlife in the surrounding forests.

Monteverde Cloud Forest Reserve, nestled in the Tilarán Mountains, is a mist-shrouded haven for biodiversity. It's a paradise for birdwatchers, with elusive species like the resplendent quetzal calling the cloud forests home. Walk across hanging bridges high in the canopy for a unique perspective of this mystical ecosystem.

Costa Rica's marine national parks, such as Cocos Island and Isla del Coco, offer world-class diving and snorkeling opportunities. Dive alongside hammerhead sharks, manta rays, and other incredible marine life in the crystal-clear waters surrounding these protected islands.

Palo Verde National Park, in the Guanacaste region, is a wetland sanctuary that hosts an astounding variety of migratory birds, making it a birdwatcher's paradise. Boat tours along the Tempisque River provide a close encounter with crocodiles, monkeys, and countless bird species.

The biodiversity found within these national parks and reserves is staggering, with countless species of mammals, birds, reptiles, amphibians, and plants awaiting discovery. Whether you're a nature enthusiast, a wildlife photographer, or simply seeking a deep connection with the natural world, Costa Rica's national parks and reserves offer an unparalleled opportunity to immerse yourself in the beauty and wonder of the country's diverse ecosystems.

In these protected areas, you can witness the intricate web of life that makes Costa Rica a global hotspot for biodiversity. Each park and reserve is a chapter in the story of this remarkable nation's dedication to preserving its natural heritage for future generations to explore and cherish.

Costa Rica's Unique Cuisine: A Tasty Fusion

Costa Rica's cuisine is a delectable fusion of flavors and influences, a culinary journey that mirrors the nation's rich cultural diversity and history. In this chapter, we'll explore the unique and mouthwatering dishes that define Costa Rican gastronomy.

At the heart of Costa Rican cuisine is the concept of "casado," which translates to "married." A casado is a traditional meal that typically includes rice, beans, meat (often chicken, beef, or fish), vegetables, and a side of salad. It's a wholesome and balanced plate that provides sustenance for the day.

Rice and beans are staples of the Costa Rican diet, often referred to as "gallo pinto" when combined. This classic dish features rice and black beans sautéed together with spices, bell peppers, and onions, creating a flavorful medley. It's often served for breakfast, accompanied by eggs and plantains.

Plantains, a type of banana, are a ubiquitous ingredient in Costa Rican cuisine. They can be served in various forms, from plátanos maduros (ripe and sweet plantains) to patacones (fried and flattened green plantains). These versatile fruits add a delightful sweetness and texture to many dishes.

Costa Rican coffee is renowned worldwide for its exceptional quality and flavor. The country's coffee plantations, nestled in the fertile highland regions, produce some of the finest arabica beans. A cup of freshly brewed Costa Rican coffee is a must-try for any coffee lover.

Seafood lovers will delight in the coastal cuisine of Costa Rica. With a long coastline along both the Pacific and Caribbean, the country offers an abundance of fresh fish and shellfish. Ceviche, a dish of marinated raw fish or seafood, is a refreshing and zesty specialty often enjoyed along the coast.

Costa Rica's love for fresh fruits is evident in the many fruit markets and stands found throughout the country. Tropical delights like mangoes, papayas, pineapples, and guavas are readily available and incredibly flavorful. You can enjoy them as a refreshing snack or in fruit salads.

One unique and beloved ingredient in Costa Rican cuisine is "Salsa Lizano." This brown, slightly sweet, and tangy condiment is drizzled over everything from rice and beans to meat and vegetables, adding a distinctive flavor that's synonymous with Costa Rican dishes.

Another specialty worth savoring is "Olla de Carne," a hearty beef stew simmered with an array of vegetables like yuca, corn, and plantains. It's a comforting and satisfying dish that showcases the country's agricultural bounty.

Costa Rican desserts often feature sweet rice puddings, tres leches cake (a sponge cake soaked in three kinds of milk), and empanadas filled with sweet ingredients like guava or dulce de leche.

For those with a penchant for adventure, you can explore the street food scene in Costa Rica. Tantalizing treats like "tamales" (steamed pockets of masa filled with meat or vegetables), "chifrijo" (a snack of beans, rice, and pork), and "empanadas" (savory turnovers) can be found at local markets and food stalls.

In summary, Costa Rican cuisine is a delightful fusion of flavors, reflecting the nation's history, geography, and cultural diversity. From savory casados to sweet tropical fruits, the country's culinary offerings are as diverse and vibrant as its landscapes. Exploring Costa Rican cuisine is not just about tasting the food; it's about immersing yourself in a rich culinary heritage that tells the story of this enchanting nation.

Must-Try Dishes and Street Food Delights

When it comes to Costa Rican cuisine, there's a delightful world of flavors waiting to be explored. In this chapter, we'll uncover some must-try dishes and street food delights that will tantalize your taste buds and give you a true taste of Costa Rica.

Let's start with the iconic "Gallo Pinto." This dish is the heart and soul of Costa Rican breakfasts. It's a simple yet flavorful combination of rice and black beans sautéed together with spices, bell peppers, and onions. Gallo Pinto is often served with eggs, tortillas, and a side of fresh fruit. It's a hearty and satisfying way to kickstart your day.

If you're looking for a classic Costa Rican lunch or dinner, "Casado" is the answer. This dish marries various elements onto one plate, just as the name suggests. A typical casado includes rice, black beans, a choice of meat (chicken, beef, or fish), vegetables, salad, and fried plantains. It's a well-balanced meal that showcases the country's staple ingredients.

For seafood enthusiasts, "Ceviche" is a must-try. This refreshing dish consists of fresh raw fish or seafood marinated in lime or lemon juice, mixed with onions, bell peppers, cilantro, and a dash of spice. It's a zesty and tangy treat, often enjoyed as an appetizer or snack along the coastal regions of Costa Rica.

When you're exploring the vibrant street food scene, be sure to sample "Tamales." These are steamed pockets of masa (corn dough) filled with a savory mixture of meat, vegetables, and spices, all wrapped in a banana leaf. Tamales are a popular snack or meal during festivals and holidays, and they come in various regional variations.

"Chifrijo" is another street food favorite. It's a delectable combination of crispy pork cracklings (chicharrones), black beans, rice, and diced tomatoes, all topped with Lizano sauce. This savory and crunchy dish is often enjoyed with a cold beer and is perfect for sharing with friends.

Empanadas are a beloved snack in Costa Rica. These savory turnovers come filled with an array of ingredients, including cheese, beans, ground meat, or vegetables. The dough is typically fried to golden perfection, creating a crispy outer shell that complements the flavorful fillings.

If you have a sweet tooth, don't miss out on trying "Arroz con Leche." This sweet rice pudding is infused with cinnamon and vanilla, creating a comforting and creamy dessert. It's often garnished with a sprinkle of ground cinnamon on top.

And speaking of sweets, "Tres Leches Cake" is a dessert you simply can't pass up. This sponge cake is soaked in a combination of three milks—evaporated milk, condensed milk, and heavy cream. The result is a moist, indulgent treat that's perfect for satisfying your sugar cravings.

As you wander the streets of Costa Rica, you'll come across various fruit vendors offering tropical delights like mangoes, pineapples, watermelons, and papayas. Enjoy them as refreshing snacks or ask for a fruit salad, often prepared with a squeeze of lime for an extra burst of flavor.

Costa Rican cuisine is not only about the dishes but also the rich tapestry of flavors and traditions that make every bite a unique experience. Whether you're savoring a plate of Gallo Pinto for breakfast, indulging in Ceviche by the beach, or munching on Tamales from a street vendor, you'll discover that Costa Rica's culinary offerings are a delicious reflection of its culture and heritage.

Coffee and Chocolate: Costa Rica's Liquid Gold

Costa Rica's coffee and chocolate are often referred to as "liquid gold," and for good reason. These two beloved exports have not only contributed to the country's economy but have also become emblematic of its culture and traditions.

Let's start with coffee, a beverage that holds a special place in the hearts of many around the world. Costa Rican coffee is renowned for its exceptional quality and flavor. The country's coffee plantations, nestled in the fertile highland regions, produce some of the finest arabica beans. The combination of the ideal climate, rich volcanic soil, and careful cultivation methods results in a coffee that's celebrated for its mild yet full-bodied taste.

The history of coffee in Costa Rica dates back to the 18th century when coffee plants were first introduced to the country. The coffee industry began to thrive, and by the 19th century, coffee had become one of Costa Rica's primary exports. Coffee cultivation played a crucial role in the country's economic development and helped fund various national infrastructure projects.

Today, Costa Rica's coffee industry is known for its commitment to sustainable and eco-friendly practices. Many coffee farms prioritize shade-grown coffee, which helps protect the diverse ecosystems in which the beans are cultivated. Additionally, the country has seen a growing interest in organic and fair trade coffee production, aligning with global trends toward responsible and ethical coffee sourcing.

Visiting a coffee plantation in Costa Rica is an enriching experience. You can witness the entire coffee production process, from the cultivation and harvesting of coffee cherries to the drying and roasting of the beans. Coffee tours often culminate in a tasting session, allowing you to savor the complex flavors and aromas of Costa Rican coffee.

Now, let's turn our attention to chocolate, another treasure of Costa Rica. While not as widely known as its coffee, Costa Rican chocolate is gaining recognition for its quality and unique flavor profiles.

Cacao has a long history in the region, with indigenous communities using it for centuries. In recent years, Costa Rica has seen a resurgence of interest in cacao cultivation and chocolate production. The country's cacao beans are known for their fruity and floral notes, which make for distinctively delicious chocolate.

Chocolate tours and tastings have become popular activities for tourists, offering insights into the chocolate-making process. You can learn about the stages of chocolate production, from harvesting cacao pods to fermenting and roasting the beans, and finally, crafting them into delectable chocolate bars and treats.

Costa Rican chocolate makers often take pride in using traditional and artisanal methods, emphasizing the quality of their cacao beans. Some even incorporate unique ingredients like local fruits, nuts, and spices to create one-of-a-kind chocolate flavors.

Whether you're sipping a cup of freshly brewed Costa Rican coffee or indulging in a square of locally crafted chocolate, you're partaking in a rich tradition that celebrates the bountiful flavors of this vibrant nation. These "liquid gold" treasures are more than just beverages and treats; they're a taste of Costa Rica's heritage and a testament to the country's dedication to excellence in agriculture and craftsmanship.

The Craft Beer and Distillery Scene

Costa Rica's craft beer and distillery scene has been brewing and distilling its own distinct identity in recent years, offering a delightful alternative to the more traditional coffee and chocolate experiences. While the country may be famous for its natural wonders and tropical delights, it's also making a name for itself in the world of craft beverages.

Craft beer has been steadily gaining popularity in Costa Rica, with microbreweries and craft beer bars popping up across the country. These passionate brewers have been experimenting with flavors, styles, and techniques to create a unique Costa Rican beer culture.

One of the reasons for the craft beer boom is the availability of high-quality, locally sourced ingredients. Many brewers take advantage of the country's crystal-clear waters, pure air, and fertile soil to produce exceptional beer. You'll find a diverse range of styles, from refreshing lagers and hoppy IPAs to rich stouts and unique tropical fruit-infused brews.

Costa Rica's craft beer community is known for its camaraderie and collaboration. Brewers often come together to share ideas and create limited-edition beers that showcase the country's creativity and innovation. Additionally, beer festivals and events have become a popular way to celebrate the craft beer scene.

Craft distilleries have also been making their mark on the beverage landscape. Some producers have turned their attention to traditional spirits like rum and aguardiente, while others have ventured into the world of craft gin and vodka. These distilleries emphasize quality and craftsmanship, often using locally grown ingredients to infuse their spirits with Costa Rican flavors.

Visiting craft breweries and distilleries in Costa Rica can be an enlightening experience. You'll have the opportunity to tour the facilities, learn about the production process, and, of course, sample some of the finest craft beverages the country has to offer. It's a chance to connect with the artisans behind the products and gain insight into their passion for creating unique flavors.

As the craft beer and distillery scene continues to grow, Costa Rica is increasingly becoming a destination for beverage connoisseurs. Whether you're exploring the bustling streets of San José or the serene landscapes of the countryside, you're likely to encounter local brewpubs and distilleries where you can savor the essence of Costa Rican craftsmanship in a glass.

The craft beer and distillery scene in Costa Rica is a testament to the nation's spirit of innovation and a reflection of its commitment to quality and taste. It's a journey worth embarking on, whether you're a seasoned enthusiast or simply looking for a refreshing and flavorful way to experience the country's culture and hospitality.

Costa Rica's Exotic Fruits and Refreshing Drinks

Costa Rica's exotic fruits and refreshing drinks are a testament to the country's abundance of tropical flavors. As you journey through the lush landscapes and vibrant markets, you'll encounter a dazzling array of fruits and beverages that are both unique and mouthwatering.

One of the most iconic tropical fruits in Costa Rica is the pineapple. Known locally as "piña," Costa Rican pineapples are renowned for their sweet and juicy flesh. You can savor them fresh, as part of a fruit salad, or even in tropical smoothies and cocktails.

Mangoes, another tropical delight, are celebrated for their luscious sweetness and vibrant colors. These juicy fruits are a common sight in Costa Rican markets and are often enjoyed fresh or blended into refreshing mango smoothies.

Papayas, with their orange flesh and sweet flavor, are a staple in Costa Rican cuisine. They're used in fruit salads, as toppings for desserts, and as a standalone snack. Papaya juice is also a popular choice for a revitalizing drink.

Costa Rica's native guava, known as "guayaba," is a unique fruit that's both fragrant and flavorful. Guavas are often turned into jams, jellies, and juices, with their distinctive taste offering a tropical twist to various dishes and drinks.

Perhaps one of the most exotic fruits you'll encounter is the "maracuyá," or passion fruit. With its wrinkled exterior and tangy, aromatic seeds, this fruit is used to make refreshing passion fruit juice, a popular and invigorating beverage.

Tamarind, locally known as "tamarindo," is another intriguing fruit. Its sour and slightly sweet pulp is often used to make tamarind juice or syrup, creating a zesty and thirst-quenching drink.

Costa Rica's refreshing drinks go beyond just fruit juices. "Agua de pipa" or coconut water is a natural and hydrating option, with fresh coconuts readily available from street vendors. Sipping coconut water straight from the fruit is a delightful way to stay refreshed.

Horchata, a sweet and creamy rice-based drink, is also a favorite among locals and visitors alike. It's often flavored with cinnamon and vanilla, creating a soothing and indulgent beverage.

And let's not forget "cerveza," or beer, which plays a significant role in Costa Rican culture. Local breweries produce a range of beers, from light lagers to hoppy ales, offering a cold and satisfying way to unwind after a day of exploration.

Costa Rica's coffee culture extends beyond a morning cup of joe. You can find "café con leche" (coffee with milk) served hot or iced, providing a delightful caffeine boost with a touch of creaminess.

For those seeking a non-alcoholic option, "refrescos naturales" are popular choices. These are fresh fruit smoothies made from a variety of fruits, often blended with water or milk for a cooling and nutritious treat.

As you travel through Costa Rica, be sure to sample these exotic fruits and refreshing drinks. They are not just a feast for the taste buds but also a way to immerse yourself in the vibrant flavors and culture of this tropical paradise. Whether you're sipping on a cool coconut water by the beach or indulging in a colorful fruit salad at a local market, you'll find that Costa Rica's culinary offerings are a delightful and refreshing experience.

Top Tourist Attractions: From Beaches to Volcanoes

Costa Rica, often referred to as the "Switzerland of Central America" for its peaceful and neutral stance in the region, is a country blessed with an abundance of natural wonders and captivating tourist attractions. In this chapter, we'll explore some of the top destinations that draw visitors from around the world to this enchanting land.

Let's start with Costa Rica's world-famous beaches. The country boasts a coastline stretching along both the Pacific Ocean and the Caribbean Sea, offering an array of beautiful beach destinations. On the Pacific side, you'll find gems like Tamarindo, Manuel Antonio, and Playa Flamingo, each with its own unique charm. These beaches are renowned for their golden sands, clear waters, and opportunities for surfing, snorkeling, and relaxation.

Over on the Caribbean coast, destinations like Puerto Viejo and Cahuita offer a different beach experience. Here, you can explore lush rainforests that meet the sea, indulge in Caribbean cuisine, and immerse yourself in the laid-back, Afro-Caribbean culture that defines this region.

Costa Rica's volcanic landscapes are another major draw. The country is home to numerous active and dormant volcanoes, each with its own allure. Arenal Volcano, in the northern region, is one of the most iconic. Visitors can witness the volcano's dramatic eruptions from safe viewing areas and soak in natural hot springs nearby.

Poás Volcano, situated near the capital city of San José, offers a unique opportunity to peer into an active volcano's crater. The sulfuric fumaroles and turquoise crater lake create a surreal and mesmerizing scene.

Costa Rica's commitment to conservation is evident in its national parks. Corcovado National Park, located on the Osa Peninsula, is often hailed as one of the most biologically diverse places on Earth. It's a haven for nature enthusiasts and wildlife lovers, with jaguars, tapirs, and macaws roaming the pristine rainforests.

Tortuguero National Park, accessible only by boat or plane, is a crucial nesting site for sea turtles. Witnessing these ancient reptiles coming ashore to lay their eggs under the moonlight is a once-in-a-lifetime experience.

Manuel Antonio National Park, on the Pacific coast, combines lush rainforests with pristine beaches. Hiking trails lead to viewpoints with breathtaking vistas, and you can encounter playful squirrel monkeys along the way.

Monteverde Cloud Forest Reserve, nestled in the Tilarán Mountains, offers a mist-shrouded sanctuary for birdwatchers and nature enthusiasts. Its hanging bridges allow you to explore the canopy and discover elusive species like the resplendent quetzal.

Costa Rica's rich cultural heritage is also on display in its historic cities. San José, the capital, is a vibrant hub with museums, theaters, and markets. It's a gateway to the country's cultural treasures and serves as a starting point for many adventures.

Cartago, the country's former capital, is known for the stunning Basílica de Nuestra Señora de los Ángeles, a significant pilgrimage site. Heredia, with its colonial architecture, offers a glimpse into Costa Rica's history.

As you journey through Costa Rica, you'll find that its top tourist attractions encompass a breathtaking variety of landscapes, from pristine beaches to towering volcanoes, lush rainforests, and vibrant cities. Whether you seek adventure, relaxation, or a deep connection with nature, Costa Rica offers a remarkable tapestry of experiences that make it a destination like no other.

A Journey into Costa Rica's Rainforests

Embarking on a journey into Costa Rica's rainforests is like stepping into a living Eden. These lush and vibrant ecosystems, which cover a significant portion of the country, are teeming with biodiversity and natural wonders that beckon explorers and nature enthusiasts alike.

The rainforests of Costa Rica are part of the broader Mesoamerican Biological Corridor, a network of protected areas spanning from Mexico to Panama. What sets Costa Rica's rainforests apart is their incredible diversity, which has earned the country the reputation of being one of the world's biodiversity hotspots.

One of the defining features of Costa Rican rainforests is their lush greenery. Towering trees with colossal buttress roots create a dense canopy that shades the forest floor. Epiphytes, such as orchids and bromeliads, cling to branches, adding bursts of color to the emerald tapestry. Mosses and ferns adorn the trunks, further enhancing the forest's enchanting beauty.

As you venture deeper into these rainforests, you'll encounter a breathtaking array of wildlife. Spider monkeys swing through the trees, their acrobatic antics a testament to their agility. Howler monkeys provide a symphony of echoing calls that reverberate through the forest, earning them the title of the loudest land animal on Earth.

Sloths, both the two-toed and three-toed varieties, move at a languid pace high in the canopy, blending seamlessly with the foliage. Keen-eyed observers may spot the elusive jaguar prowling silently in search of prey, a testament to the rainforest's role as a sanctuary for endangered and elusive species.

The avian diversity in Costa Rican rainforests is staggering. Over 900 bird species call these forests home, making it a paradise for birdwatchers. The resplendent quetzal, with its iridescent plumage, is a sought-after sight, while toucans and parrots add vibrant splashes of color to the treetops.

Costa Rica's rainforests are not just a feast for the eyes and ears but also a treasure trove of botanical wonders. Medicinal plants, used by indigenous communities for centuries, thrive amidst the undergrowth. Among them, you'll find the cinchona tree, the source of quinine, a remedy for malaria.

One of the most magical experiences in these rainforests is witnessing bioluminescence, an otherworldly phenomenon caused by organisms like fireflies and fungi. On a moonless night, the forest floor can come alive with a soft, natural glow, illuminating the path for nocturnal creatures.

Waterfalls cascade from rocky outcrops, creating tranquil pools where you can take a refreshing dip. The country's many rivers meander through the forests, offering opportunities for river rafting and kayaking adventures amidst pristine wilderness.

Costa Rica's commitment to conservation is evident in its extensive network of national parks and reserves, which protect large swathes of these rainforests. Visitors can explore these natural wonders through well-maintained trails, canopy walks, and guided tours that provide insights into the delicate balance of life within these ecosystems.

A journey into Costa Rica's rainforests is a journey into the heart of one of the planet's most biologically rich and awe-inspiring realms. It's a place where nature reigns supreme, where every rustle, chirp, and roar tells a story of survival and adaptation. These rainforests are a testament to the country's dedication to preserving its natural heritage and an invitation to all who seek to be immersed in the captivating beauty of this lush green world.

Diving into Costa Rica's Marine Treasures

Diving into Costa Rica's marine treasures is like entering a realm of unparalleled beauty and biodiversity. This tropical paradise, nestled between the Pacific Ocean and the Caribbean Sea, offers a world-class underwater experience that captivates divers and snorkelers from around the globe.

Let's begin with the Pacific coast, which is renowned for its vibrant marine life. The waters of the Pacific Ocean are rich in nutrients, creating a thriving ecosystem that's a magnet for divers. The Guanacaste region, in particular, is a hotspot for underwater exploration. Its pristine dive sites, like the Catalina Islands and Bat Islands, are teeming with marine species.

The Catalina Islands, located off the northwest coast, are famous for their rocky formations and the chance to encounter large schools of fish, including snappers, jacks, and rays. The Bat Islands are known for their thrilling encounters with bull sharks, making them a bucket-list destination for shark enthusiasts.

Further south, the Manuel Antonio National Park offers an opportunity to explore a unique marine environment. Its coral reefs are home to an array of colorful fish, sea turtles, and even occasional visits from humpback whales during their migration season.

On the Caribbean side, the waters are warmer and shelter a different range of species. The Gandoca-Manzanillo Wildlife Refuge, near the southern border with Panama, is a snorkeler's paradise. Its calm, crystal-clear waters are ideal for observing vibrant coral formations and a kaleidoscope of marine life, including angelfish, parrotfish, and seahorses.

Another Caribbean gem is Cahuita National Park, where a coral reef system stretches along the coastline. Snorkelers can explore this underwater wonderland, coming face to face with nurse sharks, rays, and a diverse array of tropical fish. The park's pristine beaches, framed by lush rainforest, make for a perfect post-dive relaxation spot.

Costa Rica also offers opportunities for encounters with some of the ocean's giants. Humpback whales migrate along the Pacific coast from July to November, and the Osa Peninsula is a prime spot to witness these magnificent creatures breaching and spouting. Meanwhile, olive ridley and leatherback sea turtles come ashore to nest along both coasts, offering a chance to witness the miracle of their life cycles.

Costa Rica's dedication to marine conservation is evident in its commitment to protecting its coastal waters and marine life. The country has established marine reserves and protected areas, ensuring the long-term health of its underwater ecosystems.

Whether you're an experienced diver or a beginner eager to explore the underwater world, Costa Rica's marine treasures offer a kaleidoscope of experiences. From thrilling encounters with sharks to peaceful drifts through vibrant coral gardens, the country's coastal waters are a testament to the natural wonders that make this nation a top destination for marine enthusiasts.

Adventure and Eco-Tourism: Thrills Await

Costa Rica, a land of astounding natural beauty, is also a playground for adventurers and eco-tourists seeking thrills and a deep connection with the environment. From soaring through the treetops on zip lines to rappelling down cascading waterfalls, this chapter delves into the heart-pounding experiences that await those who crave adventure.

Zip-lining, often referred to as "canopy tours," is a quintessential Costa Rican adventure. Imagine strapping into a harness, stepping off a platform, and whizzing through the forest canopy, high above the ground. The feeling of adrenaline surging through your veins as you glide between trees, taking in breathtaking vistas, is an exhilarating experience that's easily accessible in many parts of the country.

For those who prefer a more vertical descent, waterfall rappelling is a thrilling option. Costa Rica's rainforests are dotted with waterfalls, some towering several hundred feet. Guides will equip you with the necessary gear and guide you down these cascades, allowing you to experience the raw power of nature up close.

White-water rafting and kayaking enthusiasts will find themselves in paradise. The country's rivers offer a range of experiences, from leisurely floats through serene rainforest landscapes to adrenaline-pumping rides through churning rapids. The Pacuare River, with its world-class rapids and pristine surroundings, is a must for rafting enthusiasts.

Hiking and trekking opportunities abound in Costa Rica's national parks and reserves. Traversing the dense rainforests and ascending to volcanic peaks provide a chance to witness the country's unparalleled biodiversity. In Corcovado National Park, you can embark on multi-day treks through some of the most untouched wilderness in Central America.

Surfing aficionados flock to Costa Rica's Pacific coast, which offers a variety of breaks suitable for all levels, from beginners to advanced riders. The town of Tamarindo is a popular surf destination, known for its consistent waves and vibrant surf culture. Whether you're catching your first wave or seeking to conquer epic barrels, the waves here are sure to deliver.

Costa Rica is also a prime destination for wildlife enthusiasts. Birdwatchers can tick off their lists with sightings of rare species like the resplendent quetzal and scarlet macaw. Sloths, monkeys, and big cats are often spotted on guided wildlife tours in national parks.

Eco-tourism takes center stage in Costa Rica, where sustainability and conservation are paramount. Many lodges and resorts are dedicated to preserving the environment and offering eco-friendly experiences. Staying at these accommodations not only provides an immersive experience but also supports conservation efforts.

The country's commitment to sustainability extends to its food. Many restaurants focus on locally sourced, organic ingredients, offering a farm-to-table dining experience that's both delicious and environmentally conscious.

Costa Rica's adventure and eco-tourism options cater to all levels of thrill-seekers and nature lovers. Whether you're an adrenaline junkie looking for your next rush or an eco-conscious traveler seeking a deeper connection with the natural world, this enchanting nation has an abundance of experiences that will leave you with lasting memories and a profound appreciation for the environment.

Surfing the Waves: Costa Rica's Surfing Meccas

Surfing the waves in Costa Rica is a dream come true for enthusiasts and novices alike. With its diverse coastline along the Pacific Ocean, this tropical paradise has earned its reputation as a surfing mecca, offering some of the most consistent and exhilarating breaks in the world.

One of the standout surf destinations in Costa Rica is Tamarindo. Located on the country's northwest Pacific coast, this lively beach town is synonymous with surf culture. Its long, sandy beach offers perfect conditions for both beginners and experienced surfers. The warm waters and reliable waves make it an ideal place to learn the ropes or refine your skills.

Further down the coast, Playa Grande beckons with its world-famous waves. It's part of the Las Baulas National Marine Park, known for its nesting leatherback sea turtles. Surfers here can ride powerful waves that break over a sandy bottom, providing thrilling rides and barrels that challenge even the most seasoned surfers.

Dominical, situated on the southern Pacific coast, is another hot spot for wave enthusiasts. This laid-back town is known for its consistent surf breaks and is a popular choice for those seeking a more relaxed surf scene. The atmosphere here is characterized by barefoot surfers and beachfront yoga sessions, making it a haven for both wave riders and wellness seekers.

For those looking for a unique experience, the Nicoya Peninsula is dotted with hidden surf gems. Mal País and Santa

Teresa are renowned for their beach breaks and offbeat surf culture. You can paddle out to catch waves with the backdrop of towering coconut palms and dramatic sunsets.

Costa Rica's Caribbean coast, while less known for surfing, offers its own distinct charm. Puerto Viejo is the hub for surfers exploring this side of the country. Salsa Brava, one of the Caribbean's most famous waves, challenges even the most experienced riders with its powerful barrels.

What sets Costa Rica apart as a surfing destination is its accessibility. Surf schools and rental shops are widespread, making it easy for beginners to get started. Experienced surfers will find a variety of breaks to suit their preferences, from mellow point breaks to challenging reef breaks.

Surfing in Costa Rica isn't just about riding waves; it's a way to connect with nature. You may share the lineup with playful dolphins or spot sea turtles popping their heads above the water. The country's lush rainforests often meet the sea, creating a stunning backdrop for your surf adventures.

Costa Rica's commitment to sustainability is reflected in the surf culture. Many surf schools and accommodations prioritize eco-friendly practices, ensuring that the beauty of these coastal regions is preserved for generations of surfers to come.

Whether you're a seasoned surfer chasing epic barrels or a beginner catching your very first wave, Costa Rica's surfing meccas offer an unforgettable experience. It's a place where the rhythm of the ocean sets the pace, and the thrill of riding the waves is matched only by the natural beauty that surrounds you.

The Magic of Costa Rica's Cloud Forests

The magic of Costa Rica's cloud forests is a testament to the country's astounding biodiversity and the enchanting allure of its natural landscapes. These ethereal realms, shrouded in mist and teeming with life, offer an otherworldly experience for those who venture into their depths.

Nestled high in the mountains, Costa Rica's cloud forests are characterized by their persistent cloud cover, which blankets the canopy and understory in moisture-laden mist. This unique climate creates a haven for a diverse array of flora and fauna, some of which are found nowhere else on Earth.

One of the most iconic cloud forest destinations is Monteverde, a name synonymous with lush greenery and misty landscapes. As you wander through its trails, you'll be surrounded by a verdant world of moss-covered trees, bromeliads, and epiphytic orchids. The forest is alive with the calls of howler monkeys, the melodious songs of resplendent quetzals, and the rustling of the elusive quail dove.

The famous Monteverde Cloud Forest Reserve is not just a sanctuary for wildlife but also a place for scientific research. Its commitment to conservation and sustainable tourism has made it a model for preserving these delicate ecosystems.

Further south, the Savegre Valley is another cloud forest gem. This secluded valley boasts a wealth of avian diversity, including the strikingly colored resplendent quetzal and the vibrant fiery-throated hummingbird. The nearby Los Quetzales National Park provides ample opportunities for hiking and birdwatching, offering a chance to glimpse these rare and beautiful creatures.

San Gerardo de Dota, located in the Talamanca Mountains, is a hidden gem within the cloud forests. It's a prime location to observe the elusive and brilliantly colored quetzals, which are often spotted feeding on wild avocados in the area.

The Bosque de Paz Biological Reserve, nestled in the cloud forests of the Central Volcanic Mountain Range, offers a tranquil escape into pristine wilderness. This private reserve is home to a rich tapestry of plant and animal life, including jaguars, ocelots, and sloths.

Costa Rica's cloud forests are also a crucial part of the country's watershed, providing fresh water to communities downstream. These ecosystems play a vital role in maintaining the ecological balance and ensuring a sustainable future for the nation.

Visiting a cloud forest in Costa Rica is like stepping into a dream. The interplay of mist and light creates an atmosphere of mystique, where every twist of a trail can reveal a hidden treasure. As you hike through these enchanted forests, you'll be struck not only by their beauty but also by their importance in preserving the country's rich natural heritage. It's a reminder of Costa Rica's commitment to conservation and its determination to protect these magical landscapes for generations to come.

Costa Rica's Historic Capital: San Jose

Costa Rica's historic capital, San José, is a vibrant and bustling city that serves as the heart and soul of the nation. As the country's largest city and economic center, San José offers visitors a fascinating blend of history, culture, and modernity, providing a gateway to the diverse experiences that Costa Rica has to offer.

Founded in 1738, San José has a rich history that reflects the nation's journey from colonial times to independence and beyond. The city's layout still bears traces of its Spanish colonial heritage, with a central square known as "Plaza de la Cultura" at its core. Here, you'll find historic buildings like the National Theater, a neoclassical masterpiece that hosts a variety of cultural events and performances.

Museums abound in San José, making it a hub of cultural exploration. The National Museum, housed in a former army barracks, offers a comprehensive look at Costa Rica's history, from its pre-Columbian indigenous cultures to the present day. The Gold Museum, known for its dazzling collection of pre-Columbian gold artifacts, provides insights into the country's rich heritage.

San José's bustling markets and vibrant street life give visitors a taste of Costa Rican daily life. Mercado Central, a bustling market, is a fantastic place to immerse yourself in the local culture. Here, you can sample traditional dishes like gallo pinto and empanadas, or shop for artisanal crafts and souvenirs.

The city's neighborhoods each have their own unique character. Barrio Amón and Barrio Escalante are known for their historic architecture and lively culinary scenes. In Barrio Escalante, you can savor gourmet dishes in charming restaurants and cafés.

San José's modernity is evident in its thriving business district, known as San Pedro. This area is home to several universities, including the University of Costa Rica and the University of Latina, making it a youthful and dynamic part of the city. It's also a hub for technology and innovation, with numerous startups and tech companies.

Costa Rica's political heart is also found in San José, with the National Assembly and the Supreme Court located here. The city's residents, known as "ticos," are proud of their democratic heritage, as Costa Rica is one of the most stable and peaceful countries in the region.

While San José may not have the stunning natural landscapes that draw many visitors to Costa Rica, it serves as a vital and vibrant center that introduces travelers to the country's rich history, culture, and way of life. It's a place where the past and the present intersect, where colonial architecture meets modern innovation, and where the spirit of Costa Rica is on full display.

Exploring Alajuela: Home to the Juan Santamaría International Airport

Exploring Alajuela, a province in Costa Rica, unveils a rich tapestry of culture, history, and modernity. Situated in the heart of the country, Alajuela is home to the Juan Santamaría International Airport, the nation's primary gateway for international travelers.

Juan Santamaría International Airport, named after a national hero who played a pivotal role in the country's history, is conveniently located near the capital city of San José. It serves as the busiest airport in Costa Rica, handling millions of passengers each year. Travelers arriving here are greeted by a warm and welcoming atmosphere, setting the tone for their Costa Rican adventure.

Alajuela itself is a province that encompasses a diverse range of landscapes, from the fertile Central Valley to the lush forests of the Cordillera Central mountain range. The province is known for its agriculture, with vast coffee plantations producing some of the finest coffee beans in the world. Coffee aficionados can tour the coffee farms, gaining insights into the coffee-making process and tasting the rich flavors of Costa Rican coffee.

The city of Alajuela, the provincial capital, offers a blend of historic charm and modern amenities. Its central park, Parque Central, is a gathering place for locals and visitors alike. Here, you'll find the impressive Alajuela Cathedral, a neoclassical gem that dates back to the 19th century.

Alajuela's cultural scene is vibrant, with museums and galleries showcasing the country's artistic and historical heritage. The Juan Santamaría Museum, located near the airport, pays homage to the national hero and provides a deeper understanding of Costa Rican history.

The province is also known for its lively festivals and celebrations. The Fiesta de Palmares, one of the largest and most famous festivals in Costa Rica, takes place in Alajuela every January. It features live music, bullfights, rodeos, and a vibrant carnival atmosphere that draws crowds from all over the country.

Nature enthusiasts will find much to explore in Alajuela's surrounding areas. The Poás Volcano, one of the most accessible active volcanoes in the world, is a short drive from the city. Visitors can hike to the rim of the crater and witness the bubbling, acidic green lake below.

Alajuela is also a gateway to the Arenal Volcano, an iconic natural wonder known for its perfect conical shape. The region offers hot springs, adventure activities, and opportunities for birdwatching and hiking. The Arenal Lake, a man-made reservoir, is perfect for water sports and relaxation.

Alajuela's strategic location near the airport makes it an ideal starting point for travelers embarking on their Costa Rican journey. Whether you're venturing deeper into the province to explore its natural wonders, delving into its rich history and culture, or simply using it as a convenient stopover, Alajuela offers a taste of the diversity and warmth that define Costa Rica as a remarkable destination.

Heredia: The City of Flowers

Heredia, often referred to as "The City of Flowers," is a charming and culturally rich province in Costa Rica. Nestled in the heart of the Central Valley, it boasts a unique blend of history, nature, and modernity, making it a captivating destination for both residents and visitors.

The nickname "The City of Flowers" is well-deserved, as Heredia is known for its lush gardens, colorful blooms, and well-maintained parks. The city's residents take great pride in their gardens and green spaces, and you'll often find vibrant flowers adorning streets and plazas.

The province of Heredia is one of the smallest in Costa Rica but packs a lot of character within its borders. Its capital, the city of Heredia, is home to a historic downtown area where colonial architecture mingles with contemporary life. The Central Park, or "Parque Central," is a central gathering place where locals and tourists alike come to relax, socialize, and enjoy the beauty of the city.

Within the city limits lies the National University of Costa Rica, a prestigious institution that contributes to Heredia's vibrant atmosphere. The university campus is not only an educational hub but also a cultural one, hosting various events, exhibitions, and performances throughout the year.

Heredia's historical roots trace back to the colonial period when it was founded in the 18th century. The city's architecture reflects this history, with well-preserved churches and buildings that tell the story of its past. The

Heredia Cathedral, for instance, is a striking example of colonial architecture and serves as a centerpiece of the city.

For those interested in delving deeper into Heredia's history, a visit to the Museum of Popular Culture provides insight into the province's cultural heritage. It houses a collection of traditional costumes, tools, and artwork that offer a glimpse into Costa Rica's past.

The province's natural beauty is equally captivating. Heredia is surrounded by lush mountains, making it a gateway to numerous hiking and outdoor adventures. The Braulio Carrillo National Park, located nearby, is a haven for nature lovers, with its dense rainforests, diverse wildlife, and cascading waterfalls.

Heredia is also a hub for coffee production, and the fertile volcanic soils in the region are ideal for growing high-quality coffee beans. Coffee enthusiasts can tour local coffee plantations to learn about the coffee-making process and savor some of the world's finest brews.

As you explore Heredia, you'll encounter a warm and welcoming community that takes pride in its traditions, cultural heritage, and natural surroundings. The city's nickname, "The City of Flowers," is a testament to the beauty and charm that grace this picturesque corner of Costa Rica, making it a destination well worth visiting for those seeking an authentic and enriching experience.

Cartago: A Glimpse into Costa Rica's Religious Heritage

Cartago, a city steeped in history and tradition, provides a captivating glimpse into Costa Rica's religious heritage. Nestled in the lush Central Valley, Cartago holds a special place in the hearts of Costa Ricans as a center of devotion, pilgrimage, and cultural significance.

At the heart of Cartago lies the Basílica de Nuestra Señora de los Ángeles, a revered religious sanctuary and one of the most important pilgrimage sites in the country. The story of the basilica's origins is steeped in legend and folklore. According to popular belief, a young indigenous girl discovered a small statue of the Virgin Mary with the Child Jesus in the early 17th century, near where the basilica now stands. This discovery marked the beginning of a deep spiritual connection between the people of Cartago and their patroness, La Negrita, as the statue came to be affectionately known.

The current basilica, constructed in the 19th century, is an architectural marvel, blending elements of Byzantine and Romanesque styles. Its gleaming white façade and towering twin spires make it a striking landmark visible from miles away. Pilgrims from across Costa Rica and beyond flock to the basilica, especially during the annual celebration of La Negrita on August 2nd. The atmosphere is one of devotion and reverence as thousands gather to express their faith and gratitude.

The religious significance of Cartago doesn't end with the basilica. The city is home to several historic churches and chapels, each with its own unique story. The Church of Santiago Apóstol, for example, is one of the oldest churches in Costa Rica, dating back to the 16th century. Its modest design and historical artifacts offer a window into the country's early colonial period.

The city's devotion to religious heritage extends beyond its architecture. Cartago hosts a vibrant calendar of religious festivals, processions, and celebrations throughout the year. Semana Santa, or Holy Week, is a particularly grand affair in Cartago, with elaborate processions, reenactments, and traditional rituals that draw crowds of faithful onlookers.

Beyond its religious significance, Cartago has played a pivotal role in Costa Rica's history. It served as the country's capital for nearly three centuries before San José assumed that role. The ruins of the old Cartago Cathedral, destroyed by a series of earthquakes in the 19th century, stand as a solemn reminder of the city's tumultuous past.

Today, Cartago is a city that embraces its religious heritage while also adapting to the modern world. It's a place where history and faith intersect, where the traditions of the past continue to shape the lives of its residents. Visiting Cartago offers a profound glimpse into the enduring religious devotion and cultural richness that define Costa Rica's identity.

Puntarenas: Gateway to the Pacific

Puntarenas, known as the "Gateway to the Pacific," holds a special place in Costa Rica as a bustling coastal province that connects the country to the vast expanse of the Pacific Ocean. With its strategic location on the western coast, Puntarenas has played a pivotal role in shaping the nation's history, culture, and economy.

One of the defining features of Puntarenas is its extensive coastline. Stretching along the Gulf of Nicoya and the Pacific Ocean, it offers a diverse range of beaches and coastal landscapes. The province is renowned for its sunsets, with fiery skies painting a vivid backdrop to the tranquil waters. For many travelers, Puntarenas is the starting point for coastal adventures, from leisurely beachcombing to thrilling water sports.

The city of Puntarenas, the provincial capital, is a vibrant hub where the culture of the coast thrives. The Paseo de los Turistas, a lively boardwalk that stretches along the beach, is a focal point for both locals and tourists. Here, you can savor fresh seafood dishes, enjoy the lively atmosphere of street vendors, and take in the breathtaking ocean views.

Puntarenas has a deep-rooted maritime heritage, evident in its bustling port. The port serves as a vital trade link for Costa Rica, facilitating the import and export of goods. It's also a gateway to the country's many idyllic islands, including the Isla Tortuga, known for its pristine beaches and snorkeling opportunities.

The province is a magnet for eco-tourism and adventure seekers. Puntarenas boasts a rich natural landscape, with lush rainforests, wildlife reserves, and cloud forests nearby. The Monteverde Cloud Forest Reserve, a renowned conservation area, is within driving distance, offering a chance to explore the unique biodiversity of Costa Rica.

Sportfishing enthusiasts flock to Puntarenas, lured by the promise of deep-sea fishing in the Pacific. The waters off the coast teem with marlin, sailfish, and other prized game fish, making it a premier destination for anglers from around the world.

Puntarenas is also a gateway to some of Costa Rica's most celebrated national parks and protected areas. Manuel Antonio National Park, known for its stunning beaches and diverse wildlife, is a popular day trip for visitors staying in the province.

The province is not only a hub for tourists but also a thriving center of commerce and industry. Agriculture, including rice and sugarcane cultivation, plays a significant role in the local economy. Additionally, the port of Puntarenas facilitates the export of Costa Rican coffee, bananas, and other products to international markets.

As the "Gateway to the Pacific," Puntarenas embodies the spirit of coastal Costa Rica, with its dynamic blend of commerce, culture, and natural beauty. Whether you're exploring its historic streets, basking in the sun on its beaches, or embarking on adventurous excursions, Puntarenas invites you to experience the essence of Costa Rica's western coast.

Limón: The Caribbean Coast's Cultural Hub

Limón, located on Costa Rica's Caribbean coast, is a vibrant and culturally rich province that offers a captivating blend of history, diversity, and natural beauty. As the gateway to the Caribbean, Limón has a unique identity shaped by its Afro-Caribbean heritage, lush landscapes, and bustling ports.

The province's cultural mosaic is a testament to its historical significance as a hub for trade and immigration. In the late 19th and early 20th centuries, Jamaican and other Caribbean laborers came to Limón to work on the construction of the railroad and later in the banana plantations. Their influence is palpable in the music, cuisine, and traditions of the region.

Limón's capital, also named Limón, is a lively city where this cultural fusion comes to life. Strolling through the streets, you can hear the rhythms of calypso and reggae emanating from the local bars and cafes. The vibrant colors of Caribbean-style buildings add to the city's unique charm.

Carnival in Limón is a celebration of Afro-Caribbean culture like no other in Costa Rica. Held every October, it's a riot of color, music, and dance. The streets come alive with elaborate costumes, steel drum bands, and the infectious energy of the locals.

The natural beauty of Limón is equally captivating. The province is home to some of Costa Rica's most pristine beaches, including Cahuita, Puerto Viejo, and Manzanillo.

These beaches are renowned for their golden sands, crystal-clear waters, and lush coastal rainforests. Snorkeling and diving enthusiasts can explore the coral reefs and vibrant marine life in Cahuita National Park.

The Tortuguero National Park, located in northern Limón, is a haven for wildlife enthusiasts. It's one of the most important nesting sites for sea turtles in the Western Hemisphere, drawing visitors from around the world to witness this incredible natural spectacle.

Banana and cocoa plantations are scattered throughout Limón, contributing to the province's agricultural significance. The aroma of cocoa beans fills the air, enticing chocolate connoisseurs to explore the region's chocolate-making traditions.

The province is also home to the bustling Port of Limón, one of the largest and busiest ports in Central America. It plays a vital role in the country's trade and commerce, facilitating the export of Costa Rican goods to international markets.

Limón's rich tapestry of culture, music, and natural wonders invites visitors to experience a different side of Costa Rica. It's a place where the rhythms of the Caribbean meet the biodiversity of the rainforest, creating an atmosphere of warmth, diversity, and cultural vitality that is unique to this enchanting coastal province.

Guanacaste: Sun, Sand, and Cowboy Culture

Guanacaste, often hailed as the "Sunshine Province" of Costa Rica, is a captivating region where sun, sand, and cowboy culture seamlessly converge. Located in the northwest of the country, Guanacaste is renowned for its pristine beaches, rugged landscapes, and a heritage deeply rooted in the traditions of the sabanero, or cowboy.

When you step into Guanacaste, you'll immediately notice the difference in climate. This province boasts some of the driest and sunniest weather in Costa Rica, thanks to its location in the rain shadow of the Tilarán Mountains. The result is a landscape of arid plains, rolling hills, and an abundance of sunshine, making it a popular destination for those seeking warm weather and outdoor adventures.

Guanacaste's beaches are world-famous, offering a stunning coastline along the Pacific Ocean. Tamarindo, Playa Conchal, Playa Hermosa, and Playas del Coco are just a few of the coastal gems that draw visitors with their golden sands and clear waters. Whether you're into surfing, snorkeling, or simply basking in the sun, Guanacaste's beaches have something for everyone.

But Guanacaste is not just about beaches; it's also about embracing a cowboy culture deeply ingrained in the region's identity. Sabaneros, the local cowboys, are skilled horsemen who have shaped the province's history and traditions. The annual Fiestas Civicas in Liberia, the provincial capital, showcase Guanacaste's cowboy heritage with rodeos, bullfights, and parades.

Speaking of Liberia, this bustling city is a gateway to some of Guanacaste's most iconic attractions. The Daniel Oduber Quirós International Airport, named after Costa Rica's beloved former president, is conveniently located here, making it a major entry point for travelers to the region.

Guanacaste is also home to a collection of national parks and reserves that protect its diverse ecosystems. The Rincon de la Vieja National Park, dominated by the active Rincon de la Vieja Volcano, offers hiking trails, thermal springs, and the chance to witness volcanic activity.

Wildlife enthusiasts can explore the Palo Verde National Park, a wetland paradise that teems with birdlife, including herons, egrets, and spoonbills. The park is also a sanctuary for howler monkeys, white-faced capuchins, and crocodiles.

Guanacaste's culinary scene reflects its cultural blend, with a fusion of flavors that include dishes influenced by both Spanish and indigenous cuisines. Traditional Costa Rican dishes like gallo pinto (rice and beans) and casado (a hearty meal with rice, beans, meat, and plantains) are staples, but you'll also find local specialties like carne en palo (marinated beef cooked on a stick) and chorreadas (corn pancakes).

As you explore Guanacaste, you'll discover a land of contrasts, where the arid plains meet the lush rainforests, and cowboy culture dances with the rhythms of the Pacific coast. This province embodies the essence of Costa Rica's diversity, making it a captivating destination for those seeking sun, sand, and the rich tapestry of sabanero traditions.

Pura Vida Living: The Costa Rican Lifestyle

"Pura Vida" – it's a phrase that embodies the heart and soul of Costa Rica and its way of life. Translating to "pure life" in English, Pura Vida is more than just a saying; it's a philosophy that defines the Costa Rican lifestyle. When you step into this beautiful country, you'll find that Pura Vida isn't just a catchphrase – it's a way of living, a mindset, and a reflection of the country's culture.

At its core, Pura Vida represents a laid-back and easygoing attitude toward life. It's about appreciating the simple joys and finding happiness in the everyday moments. Costa Ricans, or "Ticos" and "Ticas" as they affectionately call themselves, embrace this outlook with open arms. They understand that life is too short to be stressed and rushed, and they take the time to savor life's little pleasures.

Costa Ricans are known for their warmth and friendliness. They greet each other with a smile and a "Pura Vida," whether they're meeting a longtime friend or a complete stranger. This welcoming spirit extends to visitors, making Costa Rica a destination where you'll feel like you're among friends from the moment you arrive.

The concept of Pura Vida is deeply intertwined with nature. Costa Rica's stunning natural landscapes, from its lush rainforests to its pristine beaches, serve as a constant reminder of the beauty and wonder of the world. Ticos and Ticas have a strong connection to their environment, and you'll often find them engaging in outdoor activities, from hiking and surfing to wildlife watching and canopy tours.

This connection to nature also extends to the country's commitment to sustainability and conservation. Costa Rica is a global leader in eco-tourism and is dedicated to preserving its biodiversity and natural resources. Its extensive system of national parks and protected areas showcases its dedication to preserving its natural heritage for future generations.

Pura Vida living also means embracing a healthy and balanced lifestyle. Costa Ricans have a diet rich in fresh fruits, vegetables, and seafood. The "casado" – a typical Costa Rican meal – often includes rice, beans, plantains, salad, and a protein source like chicken, fish, or beef. Meals are hearty but not overly indulgent, promoting a sense of well-being.

Family is at the center of Costa Rican life. Ticos and Ticas hold strong family values, and it's common for multiple generations to live under one roof. This close-knit family structure fosters a sense of community and support, making Costa Rica a place where you'll feel like you're part of a big, welcoming family.

The Costa Rican healthcare system is renowned for its accessibility and quality, contributing to a longer life expectancy and a healthier lifestyle. The emphasis on preventive care and a focus on overall well-being align with the Pura Vida philosophy.

Costa Ricans also have a strong cultural identity, with traditions that celebrate their history and heritage. Festivals, music, dance, and religious ceremonies play a significant role in their lives, allowing them to connect with their roots and share their vibrant culture with the world.

In essence, Pura Vida living is about finding harmony, gratitude, and contentment in every aspect of life. It's a reminder to slow down, appreciate the beauty around you, and focus on the things that truly matter – the people you love, the experiences you have, and the natural wonders that surround you. Costa Rica's Pura Vida lifestyle is an invitation to live in the moment, embrace positivity, and treasure the gift of life itself.

Festivals and Celebrations: A Year of Color and Tradition

Costa Rica is a country that knows how to celebrate, and throughout the year, its calendar is filled with a vibrant tapestry of festivals and celebrations that showcase the rich traditions, culture, and history of the nation. From religious processions to lively carnivals, here's a glimpse into a year of color and tradition in Costa Rica.

Semana Santa (Holy Week): The week leading up to Easter Sunday is a time of deep religious reflection and fervor in Costa Rica. Across the country, you'll witness elaborate processions, reenactments of the Passion of Christ, and heartfelt religious ceremonies. Towns like Cartago and San José come alive with religious devotion during Semana Santa.

Fiestas Civicas (Civic Festivals): Many towns and cities in Costa Rica celebrate their own civic festivals, which often include parades, rodeos, bullfights, and live music. Liberia in Guanacaste, for example, holds its Fiestas Civicas in late February, showcasing the sabanero (cowboy) culture of the region.

Carnival in Limón: Held in October, the Limón Carnival is a vibrant celebration of Afro-Caribbean culture. It's a whirlwind of color, music, and dance, with lively parades, calypso rhythms, and elaborate costumes. Limón's Carnival is a dazzling spectacle that's not to be missed.

Independence Day: September 15th marks Costa Rica's Independence Day, and the entire nation bursts into patriotic fervor. You'll see parades featuring schoolchildren dressed in traditional costumes, marching bands, and the raising of the flag. The event honors the country's declaration of independence from Spanish rule in 1821.

Día de la Madre (Mother's Day): Mother's Day in Costa Rica is a heartwarming celebration of maternal love and appreciation. It's not just a day to honor biological mothers but also grandmothers and maternal figures. Families come together to show their love and gratitude through gifts and gatherings.

Día del Padre (Father's Day): Just as mothers are celebrated, fathers are honored on their special day in June. It's a time for families to express their love and affection for fathers, grandfathers, and fatherly figures.

Christmas and New Year's: The holiday season in Costa Rica is a magical time filled with traditions. Homes are adorned with nativity scenes, and the country lights up with festive decorations. Tamales, a traditional dish made of corn dough, are a must-have during this season.

La Negrita Pilgrimage: On August 2nd, thousands of Costa Ricans embark on a pilgrimage to the Basilica of Our Lady of the Angels in Cartago to honor the revered statue of La Negrita, the country's patron saint. Pilgrims often walk for days to reach the basilica and express their devotion.

Día de la Raza (Columbus Day): Celebrated on October 12th, this holiday commemorates Christopher Columbus's arrival in the Americas. It's a day to recognize the country's diverse cultural heritage, and you'll find events and festivities throughout Costa Rica.

Fiestas Zapote: Held at the end of December in San José, Fiestas Zapote is a lively fair with amusement rides, bullfights, and traditional games. It's a fun-filled way to ring in the New Year with family and friends.

Pilgrimage to the Cartago Basilica: Every year on August 2nd, Costa Ricans from all corners of the country embark on a pilgrimage to the Basilica of Our Lady of the Angels in Cartago. Many walk for days to reach the basilica, where they pay homage to La Negrita, Costa Rica's patron saint.

These are just a few glimpses into the colorful tapestry of festivals and celebrations that make Costa Rica's calendar come alive throughout the year. Whether it's a religious procession, a lively carnival, or a heartfelt tribute to mothers and fathers, each celebration adds to the cultural richness and diversity that defines this vibrant nation.

The Art and Craftsmanship of Costa Rica

The art and craftsmanship of Costa Rica is a testament to the creativity and cultural richness of this vibrant nation. From traditional crafts passed down through generations to contemporary art that reflects the country's evolving identity, Costa Rican artistry is a captivating journey through history, tradition, and innovation.

Pre-Columbian Art: Long before the arrival of European settlers, indigenous peoples inhabited the lands that would become Costa Rica. Their art, primarily expressed through pottery and sculptures, is a window into their beliefs and way of life. Pre-Columbian artifacts, including intricately designed ceramics and stone carvings, can be found in museums across the country.

Colonial Influence: The Spanish colonial period left an indelible mark on Costa Rican art. Religious art, including paintings and sculptures, played a significant role in the visual culture of the time. Many colonial-era churches and cathedrals are adorned with exquisite works of art, showcasing the fusion of European and indigenous styles.

Oxcarts and the Sarchí Tradition: The brightly painted oxcarts of Sarchí are iconic symbols of Costa Rican craftsmanship. Skilled artisans in the town of Sarchí have been creating these ornate wooden carts for generations. Each cart is a masterpiece of hand-painted design, featuring intricate patterns and vibrant colors. They are not only functional but also works of art that have earned a place on

UNESCO's Representative List of the Intangible Cultural Heritage of Humanity.

Textile Arts: Costa Rican artisans are known for their expertise in textile arts. From intricate weaving to vibrant embroidery, textiles play a central role in the country's artistic heritage. Traditional clothing, like the colorful dresses worn by female dancers during festivals, reflects the diversity of Costa Rican regions.

Contemporary Art: The modern art scene in Costa Rica is a dynamic mix of styles and influences. Costa Rican artists, inspired by their rich cultural heritage and the beauty of their surroundings, create a wide range of works, from paintings and sculptures to multimedia installations. Museums and galleries in cities like San José and Santa Ana showcase the talent of these contemporary artists.

Handcrafted Jewelry: Costa Rican jewelry artisans are known for their use of local materials like jade, volcanic stones, and seeds to create unique and stunning pieces. These pieces often incorporate traditional designs and indigenous symbolism, making them both beautiful and culturally significant.

Woodworking and Sculpture: Costa Rican woodworkers and sculptors craft intricate pieces that capture the natural beauty and wildlife of the country. From delicate wooden figurines to larger-than-life sculptures, their works celebrate the flora and fauna that make Costa Rica so unique.

Pottery: Pottery is an ancient art form in Costa Rica, and artisans continue to create pottery that reflects both traditional techniques and contemporary designs.

Functional pottery, such as plates and bowls, as well as decorative pieces, are widely produced.

Street Art: Costa Rica's urban areas are becoming canvases for street artists who use their talents to create colorful and thought-provoking murals. San José, in particular, has embraced street art as a form of creative expression, adding a modern and vibrant dimension to the city's landscape.

Costa Rican art and craftsmanship are a celebration of the country's cultural diversity and historical roots. From the ancient traditions of indigenous peoples to the contemporary expressions of today's artists, the artistry of Costa Rica is a reflection of the nation's past, present, and future, and it continues to inspire and captivate those who encounter it.

Music and Dance: The Rhythms of Costa Rica

Music and dance are the beating heart of Costa Rican culture, a vibrant and rhythm-filled reflection of the nation's diversity and history. From traditional folk music that harks back to the days of Spanish colonization to the lively sounds of Afro-Caribbean influences, the music of Costa Rica is a captivating journey through its soul.

Traditional Folk Music: The melodies of traditional Costa Rican folk music are steeped in history and often feature Spanish and indigenous influences. The "punto guanacasteco" is a beloved folk genre, known for its lyrical storytelling and use of the marimba, a wooden xylophone-like instrument. These melodies transport listeners to the countryside, celebrating the beauty of rural life.

Marimba Music: The marimba holds a special place in Costa Rican culture. Often considered the national instrument, it's used in various musical genres, including traditional folk music and popular dance music. Its rich and resonant tones create an atmosphere of festivity and celebration during cultural events and festivals.

Afro-Caribbean Rhythms: On the Caribbean coast, the influence of Afro-Caribbean cultures is deeply embedded in the music and dance. Calypso, reggae, and soca rhythms can be heard, and these genres have contributed to the unique musical identity of the region. The lively beats of steel drums and percussion instruments make Caribbean coast festivals a whirlwind of sound and movement.

Cumbia and Salsa: Cumbia, a dance and music style with roots in Colombia, has found a place in Costa Rican culture. It's a favorite at parties and celebrations, characterized by its rhythmic drumming and accordion melodies. Salsa, with its infectious beats and passionate dance, is also popular in the country's urban areas.

Danza de los Diablitos: This indigenous tradition from the Boruca people tells the story of their resistance against Spanish conquistadors. It's a mesmerizing performance in which dancers don devil masks and intricate costumes, accompanied by traditional music, reenacting their ancestors' struggles and victories.

Festival de la Luz: Every December, the capital city of San José comes alive with the Festival of Lights. This vibrant event features colorful parades, fireworks, and, of course, music and dance. Thousands of participants dance through the streets, creating a festive atmosphere that marks the beginning of the holiday season.

Ballet Folklórico de Costa Rica: This national dance company showcases the rich diversity of Costa Rican folk dance. Through their performances, they bring to life the various regional styles and traditions, preserving and promoting the country's cultural heritage.

Modern Music: In addition to traditional genres, Costa Rica has a burgeoning modern music scene. Bands and artists explore a wide range of styles, from rock and pop to hip-hop and electronic music. The local music scene offers a platform for emerging talent to express their creativity and connect with audiences both locally and globally.

Music and dance are not just forms of entertainment in Costa Rica; they are expressions of identity, history, and cultural pride. Whether it's the sweet melodies of a marimba or the infectious rhythms of Caribbean beats, the music of Costa Rica invites everyone to join in the celebration of life, love, and the country's rich cultural tapestry.

Costa Rican Folklore and Legends

Costa Rican folklore and legends are a fascinating tapestry of stories that have been passed down through generations, blending indigenous, Spanish, and African influences. These tales offer insights into the beliefs, values, and traditions of the Costa Rican people and provide a glimpse into the rich cultural heritage of the country.

La Llorona (The Weeping Woman): La Llorona is a haunting figure in Costa Rican folklore. She is said to be the ghost of a woman who lost her children and now wanders near bodies of water, weeping and searching for them. Her story serves as a cautionary tale, warning children not to wander too close to rivers and streams.

El Cadejos: El Cadejos is a mythical creature with both benevolent and malevolent forms. The white Cadejos is seen as a protector, while the black Cadejos is a symbol of evil. These creatures are often invoked to warn children against misbehaving or wandering alone at night.

La Segua: La Segua is a ghostly woman who appears as a beautiful, seductive figure to men traveling at night. However, her true form is said to be that of a grotesque, horse-faced creature. Her legend emphasizes the importance of fidelity and serves as a reminder of the consequences of infidelity.

El Chirripó Witch: This legend revolves around a witch who is said to inhabit the Chirripó Mountains. She is known for her supernatural powers, and her story is often invoked to explain strange occurrences in the region. The tale of the Chirripó Witch reflects the mystique of the Costa Rican highlands.

El Aplastador: El Aplastador, or "The Crusher," is a terrifying figure in Costa Rican folklore. He is said to be a giant who crushes anyone who crosses his path. This legend is often used to discourage children from wandering into dangerous areas or disobeying their parents.

La Carreta sin Bueyes (The Cart Without Oxen): This eerie legend tells the story of a ghostly ox cart that roams the streets at night. It is said to be driven by the spirits of those who mistreated their oxen in life. The haunting sound of the creaking cart serves as a warning against cruelty to animals.

El Sombrerón: El Sombrerón is a mischievous character who is known for serenading young women late at night. He wears a wide-brimmed hat and carries a guitar. His antics often involve braiding the manes of horses and mules. While El Sombrerón is more of a prankster than a malevolent figure, his presence adds a touch of enchantment to the folklore of Costa Rica.

These are just a few examples of the rich folklore and legends that have been woven into the cultural fabric of Costa Rica. They serve not only as captivating stories but also as lessons and warnings, preserving the values and traditions of the Costa Rican people throughout the ages.

Family and Community: The Heart of Costa Rican Society

Family and community lie at the very heart of Costa Rican society, shaping the nation's culture, values, and way of life. In this tightly-knit Central American nation, relationships extend far beyond immediate family, and a deep sense of community is fostered through shared traditions, values, and a strong commitment to social well-being.

The Extended Family: Costa Ricans place immense importance on their extended families. It's not uncommon for multiple generations to live under the same roof or in close proximity. Grandparents often play a significant role in raising their grandchildren, passing down wisdom and traditions from one generation to the next. Family gatherings and celebrations are a regular occurrence, strengthening the bonds that tie relatives together.

Tico/Tica: Costa Ricans, affectionately known as "Ticos" (for males) and "Ticas" (for females), take pride in their national identity. This sense of belonging to a larger group reinforces the importance of community. Being a "Tico" or "Tica" is more than just a label; it's a shared identity that fosters a sense of unity and camaraderie.

Pura Vida: The phrase "Pura Vida" is more than just a saying; it's a way of life in Costa Rica. It embodies the idea of living life to the fullest, appreciating the simple pleasures, and maintaining a positive outlook. This philosophy promotes a strong sense of contentment and harmony, both within families and in the wider community.

Community Involvement: Costa Ricans are actively engaged in their communities. They participate in local events, volunteer for social causes, and take pride in contributing to the well-being of their neighborhoods. The sense of collective responsibility is evident in the country's commitment to education, healthcare, and social services.

Education and Family: Education is highly valued in Costa Rica, and parents often make significant sacrifices to ensure their children receive a good education. Families view education as a pathway to a brighter future and better opportunities, reinforcing the idea that success is a shared endeavor.

Social Safety Nets: Costa Rica has a strong social safety net that includes universal healthcare and a robust public education system. These services are seen as essential to promoting the well-being of all citizens, regardless of their socio-economic background. The country's commitment to social equality is deeply rooted in its history and culture.

Religion and Values: Religion, primarily Catholicism, plays a significant role in Costa Rican society. The values of compassion, generosity, and a strong sense of morality are central to the culture. Religious events, such as the Feast of the Virgin of Los Ángeles, bring communities together in celebration and reflection.

Sustainability and Environmental Stewardship: Costa Ricans are proud of their country's commitment to environmental conservation and sustainability. This shared value reflects a deep respect for nature and a desire to preserve the country's natural beauty for future generations.

Celebrations and Traditions: From Independence Day parades to colorful festivals celebrating local culture and traditions, Costa Ricans love to come together in celebration. These events provide opportunities for families and communities to bond and showcase their unique heritage.

In Costa Rica, the concept of family extends far beyond blood ties, encompassing the larger community and the nation as a whole. This sense of interconnectedness and shared responsibility is the foundation of Costa Rican society, fostering a culture of warmth, inclusivity, and a commitment to the well-being of all. It is this spirit of unity that truly defines the heart of Costa Rica.

Religion and Spirituality: A Multifaceted Landscape

Religion and spirituality in Costa Rica create a multifaceted landscape that reflects the nation's cultural diversity and history. The beliefs and practices that shape the spiritual life of the Costa Rican people are as diverse as the landscapes that define their country.

Catholicism: The predominant religion in Costa Rica is Roman Catholicism. Catholicism arrived with the Spanish colonizers in the 16th century and quickly became deeply ingrained in the culture. Many Costa Ricans are devout Catholics, and religious traditions and festivals are an integral part of their lives. The Feast of the Virgin of Los Ángeles is one of the most significant religious events, drawing thousands of pilgrims to the Basilica of Our Lady of the Angels in Cartago.

Protestantism: In recent decades, there has been a significant growth in Protestantism, particularly among evangelical and Pentecostal denominations. This religious shift has brought new dynamics to the spiritual landscape of Costa Rica, with Protestant churches becoming influential centers of worship and community.

Indigenous Spirituality: Indigenous peoples in Costa Rica maintain their traditional spiritual beliefs and practices. These beliefs often revolve around the reverence of nature, with spirits inhabiting natural elements such as mountains, rivers, and forests. Indigenous ceremonies and rituals continue to be an essential part of their cultural identity.

Afro-Caribbean Religions: On the Caribbean coast, Afro-Caribbean religions such as Santería and Vodou have a presence. These syncretic belief systems blend elements of African spirituality with Catholicism and indigenous traditions. Rituals and ceremonies in these religions often involve music, dance, and offerings to ancestral spirits.

Buddhism: Buddhism has also found a place in Costa Rican society, with a growing number of people embracing Buddhist practices and philosophy. There are Buddhist temples and meditation centers across the country, offering a peaceful retreat for those seeking spiritual growth and inner peace.

Religious Tolerance: Costa Rica is known for its religious tolerance. The country's constitution guarantees freedom of religion, allowing people of all faiths to practice their beliefs freely. This diversity of religious expressions fosters an atmosphere of acceptance and coexistence.

Spiritual Connection to Nature: Costa Rica's breathtaking natural beauty has a profound spiritual significance for many of its residents. The concept of "Pura Vida" extends to a deep respect for the environment, with some seeing nature as a manifestation of the divine. This spiritual connection has also fueled the country's commitment to conservation and sustainability.

Syncretism: The blending of different religious traditions is not uncommon in Costa Rica. Many Costa Ricans incorporate elements of indigenous, Catholic, and other belief systems into their spiritual practices, creating a unique and personal approach to faith.

Costa Rica's religious and spiritual landscape is a reflection of its rich cultural tapestry, where diverse beliefs coexist harmoniously. Whether through traditional Catholicism, evangelical Christianity, indigenous spirituality, or other paths, the spiritual journey in Costa Rica is as varied and vibrant as the country itself.

Costa Rican Language and Expressions

Costa Rican language and expressions offer a colorful and distinctive window into the nation's culture and identity. While Spanish is the official language of Costa Rica, the way it's spoken and the unique expressions used by Costa Ricans, often referred to as "Ticos" or "Ticas," set their speech apart from other Spanish-speaking countries.

Tiquismos: Tiquismos are Costa Rican slang or idiomatic expressions that add a local flavor to everyday speech. These phrases and sayings can be quite playful and are often used in casual conversations. For example, the phrase "mae" is a ubiquitous term used by Ticos, similar to "dude" or "buddy" in English. It's not uncommon to hear someone say, "¡Hola, mae!" as a friendly greeting.

Vos: In Costa Rica, the use of "vos" is prevalent in everyday speech. While most Spanish-speaking countries use "tú" as the informal second-person singular pronoun, Costa Ricans favor "vos." This grammatical choice, known as "voseo," is a unique feature of Costa Rican Spanish. For example, instead of saying "Tú eres amable" (You are kind), a Tico might say "Vos sos amable."

Pura Vida: Perhaps the most iconic Costa Rican expression is "Pura Vida." It's more than just a saying; it's a way of life. "Pura Vida" translates to "Pure Life," but its meaning goes beyond words. It embodies the idea of living life to the fullest, appreciating the simple pleasures, and maintaining a positive outlook. Ticos and Ticas use it to greet each other, express gratitude, or describe a laid-back lifestyle.

Estar en el ombligo del mundo: This expression, literally meaning "to be in the belly button of the world," is used to describe someone or something that is in a remote or isolated location. Costa Rica's lush rainforests and rugged terrain have given rise to this colorful phrase.

Jama: If you're in Costa Rica and you hear someone use the word "jama," they're talking about food. Whether it's a delicious meal or just a quick snack, "jama" is the go-to term for anything edible.

Tuanis: Another popular slang term, "tuanis" means something is cool, great, or awesome. For example, if you're impressed by something, you might say, "¡Eso está tuanis!" (That's cool!).

Fresca: While in other Spanish-speaking countries "fresca" means a soft drink, in Costa Rica, it's often used to refer to any type of cold beverage, including bottled water or juice.

Costa Rican Accents: Like any language, Spanish in Costa Rica has regional accents and variations. The accent in San Jose, the capital, is considered the standard accent, but you'll find variations in pronunciation and vocabulary in different regions of the country.

Costa Rican language and expressions are not only a reflection of the country's linguistic diversity but also of its laid-back and friendly culture. Learning some of these phrases and embracing the "Pura Vida" spirit can enhance your experience while exploring this beautiful nation and connecting with its warm-hearted people.

Learning Spanish: Tips for Travelers

Learning Spanish is a valuable skill for travelers visiting Costa Rica, or any Spanish-speaking country for that matter. While many Costa Ricans speak some level of English, especially in tourist areas, having a basic understanding of Spanish can greatly enhance your travel experience and open doors to authentic interactions with locals. Here are some tips to help you on your journey to learning Spanish for your Costa Rican adventure:

1. Start with the Basics: Begin with essential phrases and vocabulary. Learn common greetings, how to introduce yourself, and basic conversational expressions. This foundation will be incredibly useful in day-to-day interactions.

2. Language Apps and Online Courses: There are numerous language learning apps and online courses available that cater to all levels of proficiency. These tools offer interactive lessons and exercises to help you build your language skills at your own pace.

3. Practice Pronunciation: Spanish pronunciation can be challenging for English speakers due to its different vowel sounds and rolled "r" sounds. Practice pronunciation by listening to native speakers, and consider taking pronunciation lessons if possible.

4. Immerse Yourself: If you have the opportunity, immerse yourself in Spanish-speaking environments. Travel to local markets, engage in conversations with locals, and participate in cultural activities. Immersion is one of the most effective ways to learn a language quickly.

5. Language Classes: If you're planning an extended stay in Costa Rica, consider enrolling in language classes. Many language schools offer immersive programs where you can study Spanish intensively for several weeks or months.

6. Language Exchange: Seek out language exchange partners, both online and in person. This allows you to practice your Spanish with native speakers while helping them improve their English. It's a win-win situation.

7. Carry a Phrasebook: A pocket-sized Spanish phrasebook can be a handy companion during your travels. It provides quick reference for common phrases and vocabulary when you need them.

8. Be Patient and Persistent: Learning a new language takes time and patience. Don't be discouraged by initial challenges. Keep practicing, and you'll gradually see improvement.

9. Use Technology: Use language learning apps, podcasts, and YouTube videos to supplement your learning. These resources can provide additional exposure to the language and reinforce what you've learned.

10. Cultural Sensitivity: Along with the language, it's important to understand the cultural nuances of communication. Costa Ricans are known for their politeness and use of formal language in certain situations. Learning these cultural aspects can help you navigate social interactions more smoothly.

11. Enjoy the Process: Learning a new language is an exciting journey. Embrace the process and enjoy the sense of accomplishment as you become more proficient in Spanish.

Remember, even a basic understanding of Spanish can go a long way in Costa Rica. Locals often appreciate the effort you make to speak their language, and it can lead to more enriching and meaningful travel experiences. So, whether you're ordering "jama" (food) at a local eatery, seeking directions, or simply engaging in friendly conversations with Ticos and Ticas, your efforts to learn Spanish will enhance your adventure in this beautiful country.

Indigenous Languages: Preserving Cultural Heritage

Indigenous languages in Costa Rica are an integral part of the country's rich cultural tapestry. These languages are not just a means of communication; they are vessels of history, tradition, and identity for the various indigenous communities that call Costa Rica home.

Bribri and Cabécar: In the Talamanca region, you'll find the Bribri and Cabécar communities. These two closely related languages belong to the Chibchan language family and are among the most widely spoken indigenous languages in Costa Rica. They have unique features, such as complex verb conjugations, reflecting the intricate relationships between speakers and their environment.

Ngäbere: The Ngäbere people, also known as the Ngöbe-Buglé, inhabit areas in both Costa Rica and Panama. The Ngäbere language is part of the Chibchan family and is characterized by its distinct pronunciation and vocabulary. Efforts are being made to preserve and revitalize this language among the Ngäbere community.

Buglere: Related to Ngäbere, the Buglere language is spoken by a smaller community within the Ngäbere-Buglé ethnic group. It, too, is part of the Chibchan language family and is recognized for its uniqueness within the broader linguistic landscape.

Boruca: The Boruca people, known for their vibrant masks and indigenous art, speak the Boruca language. While it's considered critically endangered, community initiatives are underway to revitalize and document this language.

Teribe: The Teribe language, also known as Naso-Teribe, is spoken by the Teribe people in northern Costa Rica. This language is part of the Chibchan family and is characterized by its tonal aspects, which convey different meanings through pitch variations.

Brörán: The Brörán language, spoken by the Brunka people, is another indigenous language of Costa Rica. Like many indigenous languages, Brörán faces the challenge of preservation due to a dwindling number of speakers.

Preservation Efforts: The preservation of indigenous languages is a significant cultural and linguistic challenge. With globalization and the influence of dominant languages, many indigenous languages are endangered. Organizations and institutions in Costa Rica are working alongside indigenous communities to document, teach, and revitalize these languages. This includes creating dictionaries, educational materials, and language immersion programs.

Cultural Significance: For indigenous communities in Costa Rica, language is inseparable from their cultural identity. These languages convey traditional knowledge, stories, and spiritual practices. They are the keys to understanding the worldviews and histories of these communities.

Challenges: The challenges facing indigenous languages in Costa Rica are considerable. Younger generations often opt to speak Spanish as it is seen as more practical in a predominantly Spanish-speaking country. Economic and social pressures also contribute to the decline of indigenous languages.

Importance of Preservation: The preservation of indigenous languages is not just about language itself but about preserving the unique worldviews, knowledge, and heritage of indigenous communities. Efforts to protect and revitalize these languages are critical for the cultural diversity and cultural heritage of Costa Rica.

Indigenous languages in Costa Rica are not just linguistic entities; they are living representations of centuries-old cultures and histories. The ongoing efforts to preserve and revitalize these languages are a testament to the commitment of indigenous communities and the recognition of the immense value they hold in preserving cultural heritage.

Environmental Conservation: Costa Rica's Green Commitment

Costa Rica is renowned worldwide for its unwavering commitment to environmental conservation. This tiny Central American nation has earned a well-deserved reputation as a global leader in sustainable practices and eco-friendly policies. From lush rainforests to pristine coastlines, the country's breathtaking natural beauty has been the driving force behind its dedication to preserving the environment.

A Pioneer in Conservation: Costa Rica's journey towards becoming an environmental trailblazer began decades ago. In 1969, the country established the National Park Service, signaling its intent to protect its natural treasures. Today, more than 25% of Costa Rica's territory is under some form of protection, including national parks, wildlife reserves, and biological corridors.

Biodiversity Hotspot: Costa Rica's exceptional biodiversity is a testament to its commitment to conservation. Despite its relatively small size, the country is home to an astonishing variety of flora and fauna, making it one of the world's 17 mega-diverse nations. Visitors can spot rare and colorful birds, elusive big cats, and a myriad of plant species within its borders.

Carbon Neutrality: In a remarkable feat, Costa Rica aims to become carbon neutral by 2050. This ambitious goal reflects the country's dedication to reducing greenhouse gas emissions and mitigating the impacts of climate change. Costa Rica has already made significant strides in this direction by relying heavily on renewable energy sources, primarily hydroelectric power and wind energy.

Eco-Tourism: The nation's commitment to conservation goes hand in hand with its thriving eco-tourism industry. Visitors flock to Costa Rica to experience its natural wonders responsibly. Whether it's hiking through rainforests, observing sea turtles nesting on pristine beaches, or exploring vibrant coral reefs, eco-tourism in Costa Rica encourages visitors to appreciate and protect the environment.

Preservation of Rainforests: Costa Rica's rainforests are vital not only for the country but for the world. These lush ecosystems play a crucial role in absorbing carbon dioxide, producing oxygen, and supporting a plethora of wildlife. Through initiatives like the Payment for Ecosystem Services (PES) program, the country compensates landowners for preserving forests, further incentivizing conservation.

Protected Marine Areas: The commitment to conservation extends to the country's marine environments. Costa Rica has established numerous marine protected areas to safeguard its rich coastal ecosystems, including coral reefs and vital breeding grounds for marine species. These efforts aim to counter the threats of overfishing and habitat degradation.

Sustainable Agriculture: Costa Rica is also making strides in sustainable agriculture. Organic farming practices and responsible land use are promoted to reduce the negative impact of agriculture on the environment. Efforts are made to minimize pesticide use and protect the country's fertile soils.

Conservation Education: Education plays a pivotal role in Costa Rica's environmental efforts. Schools and organizations are dedicated to teaching the next generation about the importance of conservation. Visitors can also engage in educational programs and workshops that promote sustainable practices.

Community Involvement: The success of Costa Rica's conservation initiatives is often attributed to the involvement of local communities. Many conservation programs are community-based, ensuring that those who live in and around protected areas are actively engaged in their preservation.

Costa Rica's green commitment is not just a policy; it's a way of life deeply ingrained in the culture and values of its people. The country's dedication to preserving its natural heritage serves as an inspiration and a model for environmental conservation worldwide. Costa Rica has proven that a harmonious coexistence between humans and nature is not only possible but essential for a sustainable future.

Sustainable Tourism: A Model for the World

Costa Rica's approach to sustainable tourism has not only set an example for the world but has also redefined the way countries can balance the benefits of tourism with environmental conservation and cultural preservation.

A Paradigm Shift: In the past, many destinations viewed tourism as a double-edged sword. While it brought economic opportunities, it often led to environmental degradation and cultural erosion. Costa Rica challenged this paradigm by demonstrating that tourism could be a catalyst for positive change.

Ecotourism Emergence: The concept of ecotourism gained traction in Costa Rica in the 1980s. The idea was simple yet revolutionary: visitors could experience the country's stunning natural beauty while actively contributing to its preservation. This shift in mindset led to the development of eco-lodges, nature tours, and activities that emphasized education and conservation.

National Park System: Costa Rica's commitment to preserving its natural treasures is reflected in its extensive national park system. These protected areas not only serve as havens for biodiversity but also as prime destinations for tourists seeking to immerse themselves in the country's pristine landscapes. The Monteverde Cloud Forest Reserve and Manuel Antonio National Park are just a couple of examples of these ecotourism gems.

Community Involvement: Sustainable tourism in Costa Rica extends beyond national parks. Local communities play a crucial role in this model. Many rural areas have embraced tourism as a means of economic development. They offer homestays, guided tours, and locally sourced meals, providing visitors with authentic experiences while benefiting directly from tourism revenue.

Wildlife Conservation: The country's commitment to wildlife conservation is a hallmark of its sustainable tourism efforts. Costa Rica is home to numerous rescue and rehabilitation centers that care for injured or orphaned animals, including sloths, monkeys, and sea turtles. Visitors can observe these efforts and learn about wildlife conservation first-hand.

Certification Programs: To ensure that accommodations, tour operators, and other tourism-related businesses adhere to sustainable practices, Costa Rica developed certification programs such as the Certification for Sustainable Tourism (CST). These programs evaluate businesses based on their environmental, social, and economic impact, allowing tourists to make informed choices.

Renewable Energy: Costa Rica's reliance on renewable energy sources, particularly hydroelectric power, has made it a leader in the fight against climate change. The country's commitment to green energy aligns with the principles of sustainable tourism, attracting environmentally conscious travelers.

Educational Initiatives: Sustainability education is woven into the fabric of Costa Rica's tourism industry. Visitors can participate in guided tours and workshops that shed light on conservation efforts, environmental stewardship, and local culture. This educational aspect fosters a sense of responsibility among tourists.

Balancing Growth: The challenge for Costa Rica is to maintain this delicate balance between tourism growth and environmental conservation. Careful planning and sustainable practices are essential to prevent overdevelopment and preserve the natural and cultural assets that draw visitors in the first place.

Costa Rica's model of sustainable tourism has proven that a nation can thrive economically while safeguarding its environment and cultural heritage. It's a shining example for the world, demonstrating that tourism can be a force for good, contributing to conservation efforts, empowering communities, and educating travelers about the importance of protecting our planet.

Health and Wellness in Costa Rica

Costa Rica's commitment to health and wellness is deeply intertwined with its unique natural surroundings and cultural values. The country's dedication to providing opportunities for physical and mental well-being has made it a sought-after destination for travelers seeking rejuvenation and tranquility.

Nature's Sanctuary: One of the cornerstones of health and wellness in Costa Rica is its stunning natural environment. From pristine beaches to lush rainforests and serene mountains, the country offers a natural sanctuary for those looking to escape the stresses of modern life. The tranquil landscapes provide a serene backdrop for relaxation and self-care.

Pura Vida Lifestyle: At the heart of Costa Rica's wellness ethos is the "Pura Vida" lifestyle. Translating to "pure life," this phrase encapsulates the country's emphasis on simplicity, gratitude, and living in the moment. Visitors often find that immersing themselves in this mindset helps reduce stress and promotes overall well-being.

Yoga and Mindfulness: Costa Rica is a hub for yoga and mindfulness retreats. Many wellness centers and eco-lodges offer yoga classes in idyllic settings, allowing participants to connect with their inner selves while surrounded by the beauty of nature. These practices help reduce stress and promote mental clarity.

Spas and Wellness Centers: Costa Rica boasts a growing number of world-class spas and wellness centers. Whether it's a luxurious spa nestled in the rainforest or a serene wellness retreat overlooking the ocean, visitors can indulge in a wide range of treatments, including massages, facials, and holistic therapies.

Hot Springs: The country's volcanic landscape provides a unique opportunity for relaxation in natural hot springs. Places like Arenal and Tabacon offer visitors a chance to soak in warm, mineral-rich waters while gazing at the surrounding lush scenery. These thermal springs are believed to have therapeutic properties.

Healthy Cuisine: Costa Rican cuisine emphasizes fresh and wholesome ingredients, making it a natural fit for health-conscious travelers. Traditional dishes often feature lean proteins, fresh fruits, vegetables, and grains. The country's diverse cuisine caters to various dietary preferences, including vegetarian and vegan options.

Outdoor Activities: For those who prefer an active approach to well-being, Costa Rica offers a plethora of outdoor activities. Hiking through rainforests, surfing on Pacific waves, and zip-lining through canopies provide opportunities for exercise, adventure, and a deeper connection with nature.

Holistic Healing: Some wellness centers in Costa Rica incorporate holistic healing practices like acupuncture, reiki, and herbal remedies into their offerings. These alternative therapies are aimed at promoting physical and spiritual balance.

Eco-Friendly Practices: Many wellness retreats and eco-lodges in Costa Rica are committed to sustainable and eco-friendly practices. They prioritize environmentally friendly initiatives, such as organic farming, recycling, and reducing their carbon footprint, aligning with the principles of overall well-being and planet-conscious living.

Local Culture and Traditions: Exploring the local culture can also be a source of well-being. Engaging with Costa Rican traditions, such as folk music and dance, can provide insights into the country's rich heritage and foster a sense of connection and fulfillment.

Adventure and Relaxation: Costa Rica's wellness offerings encompass a wide spectrum, from thrilling adventures to tranquil escapes. Travelers can balance adrenaline-pumping activities with moments of serenity, creating a holistic approach to health and wellness.

Costa Rica's commitment to health and wellness extends beyond the physical, encompassing mental, emotional, and spiritual well-being. It's a place where individuals can find balance, rejuvenation, and a deep connection with themselves and the natural world—a true haven for those seeking to enhance their overall quality of life.

Education and Innovation: Costa Rica's Knowledge Economy

Costa Rica's commitment to education and innovation has transformed it into a regional leader with a thriving knowledge-based economy. The nation's investment in education, technological advancement, and research has not only propelled its own development but has also attracted global attention as a model for sustainable growth.

Educational Excellence: Education is highly valued in Costa Rica. The country boasts a strong and accessible education system, with free and compulsory primary and secondary education. The literacy rate hovers around 97%, a testament to the emphasis on learning from an early age.

Investment in Higher Education: Costa Rica places a significant emphasis on higher education. It's home to several prestigious universities, including the University of Costa Rica (UCR), which consistently ranks among the top universities in Latin America. These institutions offer a wide range of programs, including engineering, science, business, and the arts.

Technological Hub: The nation's capital, San Jose, is often referred to as the "Silicon Valley of Central America" due to its growing technology sector. The city has become a hub for technology startups and innovation, drawing in entrepreneurs and investors from around the world.

Sustainable Practices: Education in Costa Rica extends beyond traditional classrooms. The country's commitment to environmental sustainability and conservation is woven into the education system. Students often engage in projects and initiatives that promote eco-conscious practices and biodiversity conservation.

Bilingualism: Costa Rica places a strong emphasis on bilingual education. English is taught from a young age, making it a bilingual nation where many residents are fluent in both Spanish and English. This linguistic skill has contributed to its attractiveness as an outsourcing destination for customer service and technology companies.

Innovation Ecosystem: The country has nurtured a dynamic innovation ecosystem that supports startups and research initiatives. Organizations like Costa Rica's National Center for High Technology (CeNAT) and the Costa Rican Investment Promotion Agency (CINDE) provide resources and incentives to encourage innovation and foreign investment.

Environmental Technologies: Given its commitment to environmental conservation, Costa Rica is also at the forefront of environmental technologies. The nation invests in research and development of sustainable technologies, such as renewable energy, waste management, and water purification systems.

Global Partnerships: Costa Rica actively engages in international collaborations in the fields of science and technology. It's a member of international organizations and initiatives that promote research and development, furthering its position in the global knowledge economy.

Foreign Investment: The country's knowledge-based economy has attracted foreign investment from multinational corporations seeking to leverage Costa Rica's skilled workforce and technological infrastructure. This investment has spurred economic growth and job creation.

Intellectual Property Protection: Strong intellectual property protection laws safeguard innovations and inventions, encouraging companies and individuals to invest in research and development without fear of intellectual property theft.

Economic Diversification: Costa Rica's knowledge-based economy has contributed to economic diversification beyond traditional sectors like agriculture and tourism. It has helped the nation weather economic challenges and provides a stable foundation for future growth.

Costa Rica's journey from an agrarian economy to a knowledge-based one showcases the transformative power of education, innovation, and a commitment to sustainability. Its success story serves as an inspiration for countries striving to develop their own knowledge economies, demonstrating that investment in education and technology can drive progress while preserving the natural environment.

Investment and Business Opportunities

Costa Rica has emerged as a prime destination for investment and business opportunities in Central America. Its strategic location, stable political environment, educated workforce, and commitment to sustainability make it an attractive choice for both local and international investors looking to expand their ventures.

Strategic Location: Situated in the heart of Central America, Costa Rica serves as a gateway to the region. Its well-developed infrastructure, including modern ports and airports, facilitates the movement of goods and services, making it an ideal base for companies looking to access markets throughout Central America and beyond.

Stable Political Environment: Costa Rica is renowned for its political stability. It has a long-standing tradition of democracy, peaceful transitions of power, and a commitment to the rule of law. Investors appreciate the predictability and security that this stable political climate provides.

Free Trade Agreements: Costa Rica has an extensive network of free trade agreements (FTAs) that offer businesses preferential access to key markets. The Central American Free Trade Agreement (CAFTA-DR), for example, provides duty-free access to the United States, one of its largest trading partners.

Investment Incentives: The Costa Rican government actively encourages foreign investment. It offers various incentives, such as tax exemptions and grants, to attract companies in strategic sectors like technology, manufacturing, and renewable energy.

Skilled Workforce: Costa Rica boasts a well-educated and bilingual workforce. Its universities and technical institutes produce a steady stream of graduates in fields like engineering, information technology, and business, meeting the demands of a growing knowledge-based economy.

Technology Hub: The country's burgeoning technology sector has earned it the nickname "Silicon Valley of Central America." Companies in industries ranging from software development to biotechnology have found a welcoming home in Costa Rica, drawn by its skilled workforce and supportive ecosystem.

Renewable Energy: Costa Rica is a global leader in renewable energy production. With a commitment to environmental sustainability, the nation generates a significant portion of its electricity from clean sources like hydroelectric, wind, and solar power. This not only reduces business operating costs but also aligns with sustainability goals.

Tourism: The tourism industry continues to thrive, offering investment opportunities in hospitality, real estate, and related services. The country's natural beauty, diverse landscapes, and commitment to eco-tourism make it a popular destination for travelers, creating a steady flow of visitors and potential customers.

Sustainable Practices: Costa Rica's dedication to sustainability extends to business practices. Many companies prioritize environmental responsibility, adopting eco-friendly operations and contributing to the nation's green reputation.

Access to Markets: Costa Rica's strategic location provides easy access to markets in North and South America. The country's extensive network of trade agreements facilitates exports and imports, making it an ideal base for companies engaged in international trade.

Medical Tourism: The healthcare sector, including medical tourism, is also on the rise. Costa Rica's world-class medical facilities and skilled healthcare professionals attract patients from around the world, offering investment opportunities in this growing industry.

Quality of Life: Costa Rica consistently ranks high in quality-of-life indices. Its stable healthcare system, excellent education, and pristine natural environment make it an appealing destination for professionals and their families, further enhancing the talent pool for businesses.

In summary, Costa Rica's investment and business opportunities are a testament to its commitment to economic development, sustainability, and a high quality of life. Whether you're a local entrepreneur or an international investor, this vibrant and dynamic nation offers a range of prospects across various sectors, making it an attractive destination for those seeking to grow and prosper in Central America.

Getting Around Costa Rica: Transportation Tips

Navigating the beautiful landscapes and diverse regions of Costa Rica requires an understanding of the transportation options available in this vibrant country. Whether you're a tourist exploring the lush rainforests or a business traveler attending meetings in the bustling capital, knowing how to get around Costa Rica efficiently is essential.

Roads and Highways: Costa Rica has an extensive network of roads and highways that connect cities and towns. The quality of these roads can vary, with major routes typically well-maintained, while more remote areas may have rougher terrain. The Pan-American Highway runs through the country, providing access to both the northern and southern borders.

Renting a Car: For the ultimate freedom to explore at your own pace, renting a car is a popular option. Major international rental companies operate at airports and in urban areas. Keep in mind that some remote areas may require a four-wheel-drive vehicle due to challenging terrain.

Public Buses: Costa Rica's public bus system is extensive and affordable. Buses are a common mode of transportation for locals and tourists alike. They can take you to various destinations within the country, including popular tourist spots. While buses are economical, they may not always run on a strict schedule.

Taxis: Taxis are readily available in cities and tourist areas. They are a convenient option for shorter trips or when you don't want to drive yourself. Be sure to use licensed taxis with official markings for safety and reliability.

Domestic Flights: If you need to cover long distances quickly, domestic flights are an excellent choice. Costa Rica has several domestic airports that serve major cities and popular tourist destinations. This option saves time and allows you to experience the country from a different perspective.

Shuttles: Shuttle services are common for transporting tourists between popular destinations. They offer a convenient way to travel without the hassle of driving or navigating public transportation. You can book shuttle services through tour operators or hotels.

Ferries: Given Costa Rica's Pacific and Caribbean coastlines, ferries are a vital part of the transportation system. They provide access to islands and remote coastal areas. Schedules and routes vary, so it's advisable to check in advance.

Trains: While Costa Rica has a limited passenger train system, there are scenic train rides available, such as the "Pacific Railroad" that takes you through picturesque landscapes.

Cycling: Cycling enthusiasts can explore the country on two wheels. Costa Rica has designated cycling routes, and many cities are becoming more bike-friendly.

Safety Precautions: It's important to exercise caution when traveling in Costa Rica. While the country is generally safe, be aware of road conditions, drive carefully, and secure your belongings, especially when using public transportation.

Language: Most transportation personnel in Costa Rica understand basic English, but it's helpful to know some Spanish phrases, particularly in more remote areas.

Traffic and Navigation Apps: GPS and navigation apps can be incredibly useful for finding your way around. Consider downloading offline maps before your trip to ensure you have access to directions even in areas with limited connectivity.

In conclusion, getting around Costa Rica offers various options to suit your preferences and travel needs. Whether you prefer the independence of renting a car, the convenience of public transportation, or the speed of domestic flights, this diverse country has a transportation solution for everyone. Understanding your options and planning ahead will ensure a smooth and enjoyable journey through the stunning landscapes of Costa Rica.

Planning Your Costa Rican Adventure: Practical Advice

Embarking on your Costa Rican adventure is an exciting prospect, and careful planning can make your trip more enjoyable and hassle-free. From understanding the climate to managing your budget, here's some practical advice to help you make the most of your journey.

1. Choose the Right Time to Visit: Costa Rica's climate varies significantly by region and time of year. The country has two main seasons: the dry season (December to April) and the rainy season (May to November). The best time to visit depends on your preferences, whether you prefer sunny days or lush green landscapes.

2. Create an Itinerary: Determine the places you want to visit and create a rough itinerary. Research the attractions and activities available in each region to make the most of your time.

3. Budget Wisely: Costa Rica can be relatively expensive, especially in tourist areas. Plan your budget accordingly, and be prepared for higher costs for accommodations and dining in popular destinations.

4. Pack Smart: Given the diverse landscapes, it's essential to pack a variety of clothing, from beachwear to layers for cooler regions. Don't forget essentials like sunscreen, insect repellent, and a reusable water bottle.

5. Accommodation: Research and book accommodations in advance, especially during peak tourist seasons. Costa Rica offers a range of options, from luxurious resorts to budget-friendly hostels.

6. Vaccinations and Health Precautions: Check with your doctor regarding vaccinations and health precautions for Costa Rica. Mosquito-borne illnesses like Zika and dengue are a concern in some areas, so take necessary precautions.

7. Currency: The official currency is the Costa Rican Colón (CRC), but US dollars are widely accepted. It's a good idea to carry a mix of both for convenience.

8. Transportation: If you plan to rent a car, make reservations in advance. If using public transportation, familiarize yourself with schedules and routes.

9. Safety: Costa Rica is considered one of the safer countries in Central America, but it's essential to stay vigilant. Be cautious with your belongings, avoid displaying expensive items, and be aware of your surroundings.

10. Language: While many Costa Ricans speak some English, learning a few basic Spanish phrases can enhance your experience and help with communication.

11. Activities and Tours: Research and book tours or activities you're interested in ahead of time, especially if you have specific experiences in mind, like zip-lining through the rainforest or visiting a particular national park.

12. Travel Insurance: Consider purchasing travel insurance that covers unexpected events, such as trip cancellations, medical emergencies, or lost luggage.

13. Respect the Environment: Costa Rica places a strong emphasis on environmental conservation. Follow Leave No Trace principles, dispose of waste properly, and respect wildlife.

14. Cultural Etiquette: Learn about Costa Rican customs and etiquette. Tipping is customary, and it's polite to greet people with "hola" or "buenos días."

15. Enjoy the Pura Vida: Embrace the Costa Rican philosophy of "Pura Vida," which means "pure life" or "simple life." It's about living in the moment, appreciating nature, and enjoying life to the fullest.

Planning your Costa Rican adventure is all about striking the right balance between adventure and relaxation. With these practical tips in mind, you'll be well-prepared to savor every moment of your journey in this captivating and diverse country.

Epilogue

In this epilogue, we reflect on the journey through the pages of this book, a journey that has taken us deep into the heart of Costa Rica, exploring its rich history, diverse landscapes, vibrant culture, and the warm-hearted people who call this country home. As we come to the end of our literary voyage, let's take a moment to summarize the essence of what makes Costa Rica truly exceptional.

Costa Rica, often referred to as the "Switzerland of Central America" for its stable democracy and commitment to peace, has a remarkable story to tell. We delved into its pre-Columbian history, uncovering the fascinating legacies of indigenous peoples who inhabited these lands long before Columbus arrived. We witnessed the influence of Spanish colonialism and the struggle for independence that eventually led to the modern nation we see today.

This book has been a gateway to Costa Rica's breathtaking geography, from lush rainforests teeming with wildlife to towering volcanoes and pristine beaches. We explored its national parks and reserves, each a sanctuary for the incredible biodiversity that defines this nation. And we marveled at the delicate balance between environmental conservation and sustainable tourism, a model for the world to follow.

Cuisine became an integral part of our journey as we discovered the unique flavors of Costa Rican dishes, from gallo pinto to ceviche. We raised our glasses to the country's famous coffee and explored its emerging craft beer scene. And we savored exotic fruits and refreshing drinks that are a testament to the country's fertile soil. The chapters on tourism showcased the top attractions, from beaches to volcanoes, and highlighted the adventures that await in the rainforests, cloud forests, and the depths of the ocean. We rode the waves in world-renowned surf spots, immersed ourselves in the magic of cloud forests, and dived into marine treasures beneath crystal-clear waters.

Our exploration didn't stop at the natural wonders; we also immersed ourselves in the culture and traditions of Costa Rica. We danced to the rhythms of local music, learned about folklore and legends, and gained an appreciation for the importance of family and community in Costa Rican society.

In the midst of it all, we uncovered the heart of Costa Rica—its people. Their warmth, hospitality, and the embodiment of "Pura Vida" left an indelible mark on our journey. We witnessed their devotion to religious and spiritual beliefs, their dedication to preserving indigenous languages, and their commitment to environmental conservation.

This epilogue brings us full circle, inviting you to reflect on the incredible tapestry of experiences that Costa Rica offers. It's a country that has embraced democracy and environmental stewardship while celebrating its cultural diversity and natural beauty. As you close this book, may you carry with you the essence of Costa Rica—a place where "Pura Vida" isn't just a saying; it's a way of life. And perhaps, like us, you'll find yourself yearning to return to this paradise in Central America, where every moment is an opportunity to embrace the pure and simple joys of life.